The Best of **Mr. Food**®
15-Minute Favorites

"With never any more than 15 minutes of hands-on prep time, you can have mouth-watering recipes to the table in no time flat!
'OOH IT'S SO GOOD!!'"

Grilled Jerk Chicken and
Sugared Asparagus, pages
43 and 91

Italian BLT Bread Salad,
page 123

Sweet 'n' Savory Pizza,
page 26

The Best of Mr. Food®
15-Minute Favorites

Oxmoor House®

©2004 by Oxmoor House, Inc.
Book Division of Southern Progress Corporation
P.O. Box 2463, Birmingham, Alabama 35201

ISBN: 0-8487-2753-3
ISSN: 1534-5505
Library of Congress Control Number: 2004105638

Printed in the United States of America
Second Printing 2004

Mr. Food® and OOH IT'S SO GOOD!! are registered marks owned by Ginsburg Enterprises Incorporated.

Ginsburg Enterprises Incorporated
  Chief Executive Officer: Art Ginsburg
  Chief Operating Officer: Steven Ginsburg
  Vice President, Publishing: Caryl Ginsburg Fantel
  Vice President, Creative Business Development: Howard Rosenthal
  Vice President, Sales and Licensing: Thomas R. Palombo
  Director of Finance and Administration: Chester Rosenbaum

Oxmoor House, Inc.
  Editor in Chief: Nancy Fitzpatrick Wyatt
  Executive Editor: Susan Carlisle Payne
  Art Director: Cynthia Rose Cooper
  Copy Chief: Allison Long Lowery

THE BEST OF MR. FOOD® 15-MINUTE FAVORITES, featuring the recipes of Mr. Food, Art Ginsburg
  Editor: Kelly Hooper Troiano
  Copy Editor: Donna Baldone
  Editorial Assistant: Terri Laschober
  Designer: Kelly Davis
  Director, Test Kitchens: Elizabeth Tyler Luckett
  Assistant Director, Test Kitchens: Julie Christopher
  Test Kitchens Staff: Kristi Carter, Nicole L. Faber, Kathleen Royal Phillips,
    Jan A. Smith, Elise Weis, Kelley Self Wilton
  Senior Photographer: Jim Bathie
  Photographer: Brit Huckabay
  Senior Photo Stylist: Kay E. Clarke
  Photo Stylist: Ashley J. Wyatt
  Director of Production: Phillip Lee
  Associate Production Manager: Leslie Wells Johnson
  Production Assistant: Faye Porter Bonner
  Color Specialists: Jay Parker and Jim Sheetz

  Contributor:
  Indexer: Mary Ann Laurens

Cover: *Dark Chocolate-Mint Brownies, page 199*

Contents

Welcome!!

"Straight from my kitchen comes a new collection of my fastest recipes ever! Whether the recipe is quick-cook or no-cook, you can have dinner on the table in record time. With over 160 mouthwatering recipes, you'll never spend more than 15 minutes of hands-on prep time on any of them. Discover my handy-dandy time-savin' tips throughout these pages—guaranteed to make cooking a cinch! As always, each page is filled with easy-to-find ingredients, numbered step-by-step directions, plus prep and cook times. Be sure to check out the following pages that are packed with super-duper information for saving time in the kitchen, including 10 of my favorite speedy side-dish companions. With smart use of convenience products and your time, my philosophy shines through: Quick-and-easy cooking doesn't have to sacrifice flavor! Enjoy!"

Mr. Food

Speed Cooking 101

Look to these handy-dandy guides to help you shop and cook quicker and smarter. We've even included suggestions for super-speedy sides to round out your meals—fast!

Shopping and Planning Tips

- Buy shrimp already peeled, deveined, and even cooked if you prefer. One pound raw shrimp in shells equals ¾ pound peeled raw or ½ pound peeled, cooked, and deveined.

- Buy frozen diced cooked chicken breasts or a whole deli-roasted chicken.

- Purchase fresh pasta. It cooks in half the time of dried pasta.

- Buy precut and prewashed vegetables and fruit to save chopping and cleaning time. Find them in the produce section as well as on the salad bar.

- Use minced jarred garlic. A half teaspoon of minced garlic equals 1 regular-sized clove.

- Chop and freeze ½-cup portions of bell peppers, onions, and parsley in heavy-duty, resealable plastic freezer bags—they'll be ready when you are.

- Freeze additional prepared bread-crumbs and toasted nuts in heavy-duty, resealable plastic freezer bags, too.

- Alphabetize your spices and seasonings in the cupboard—they'll be easier to find.

- Utilize the "meanwhile" method of cooking. While a portion of the recipe bakes, microwaves, simmers, or stands, use that time to prepare another part of the recipe.

- Remember 1 or 2 sides is all you need to round out your meal—keep it simple.

Meats in Minutes

For busy weeknights, here's a list of cuts that will have you in and out of the kitchen in no time.

Beef
- ground round
- flank steak
- sirloin steak
- tenderloin steak
- top round steak

Veal
- cutlet
- loin chop

Lamb
- loin chop
- leg of lamb, cubed

Pork
- boneless loin chop
- center loin chop
- cutlet
- tenderloin

Top 10 Ways Equipment Can Save Time

1 Measure dry ingredients before wet ones so you can use the same measuring cups and spoons—this eliminates washing between measuring.

2 Keep cooking utensils you use most often near the stove for handy use.

3 Keep a food chopper on the countertop to make short work of chopping vegetables.

4 Use a pizza cutter to cut dough or to cut day-old bread into cubes for croutons—it's faster than using a knife.

5 Make kitchen shears your best friend. They're ideal for chopping tomatoes in a can, snipping fresh herbs, cutting bread, and trimming skin and fat from chicken or meat.

6 Boil water faster by placing your saucepan over high heat and covering it.

7 Use your microwave to jump-start your cooking. Use it to thaw and reheat foods, and it's excellent for cooking vegetables and bacon.

8 Line with aluminum foil for easy cleanup when cooking meat, chicken, fish, or vegetables in the oven.

9 Dust off your slow cooker! No attendance is required while cooking, and supper can be ready as soon as you walk in the door.

10 Cook on the grill—especially a gas one. It not only saves time and cleanup but the smoke also flavors the food.

Super-Speedy Sides

Asparagus—Drizzle with olive oil and sprinkle with salt and pepper; then roast at 425° for 8 minutes.

Broccoli—Steam and then top with a little flavored mustard, melted butter, and a spritz of lemon juice.

Carrots—Season steamed slices with honey and tarragon.

Coleslaw—Mix preshredded cabbage with chopped apples and poppy seed dressing.

Corn—Add salsa and a pinch of ground cumin to hot, cooked whole kernel corn.

Eggplant—Marinate slices in balsamic vinegar and grill alongside the entrée.

Mashed potatoes—Stir minced garlic, chopped chives, or shredded cheese into cooked instant or refrigerated mashed potatoes.

Pineapple slices—Brush with a honey-cinnamon mixture and broil or grill.

Spinach—Stir oregano and feta cheese into cooked chopped spinach.

Tomatoes—Toss wedges with balsamic vinegar, ground pepper, and chopped fresh basil. Or top slices with crumbled feta cheese.

Party Hearty in a Hurry

❝You'll be ready to throw together a party in an instant with these crowd-pleasin' appetizers and beverages.**❞**

Roasted Pepper Salsa

2½ cups

prep: 13 minutes   chill: 30 minutes

1   (14.5-ounce) can chunky pasta-style
        tomatoes, undrained
⅔   cup drained finely chopped jarred
        roasted red bell peppers
2   large green onions, thinly sliced
¼   cup finely chopped fresh cilantro or
        fresh parsley
2   cloves garlic, minced
1   to 2 teaspoons hot sauce

1 Combine all ingredients, stirring well.
Cover and chill at least 30 minutes.
Store in refrigerator up to 3 days in an
airtight container. Serve with tortilla
chips.

Pepper News

Look for jars of roasted red bell peppers in the condiment aisle of your supermarket. They come packed in oil or water. They're a convenient alternative to roasting your own.

Corn 'n' Black Bean Salsa

4 cups

prep: 12 minutes   chill: 30 minutes

1   (15-ounce) can black beans, rinsed
      and drained
1   cup frozen corn kernels, thawed
½   cup chopped red bell pepper
½   cup chopped fresh cilantro
8   green onions, thinly sliced
3   tablespoons lime juice
2   tablespoons balsamic vinegar
½   teaspoon ground cumin
¼   teaspoon salt

1 Combine all ingredients. Cover and chill at least 30 minutes. Store in refrigerator up to 3 days in an airtight container. Serve with tortilla chips.

TIME-SAVIN' TIP

To thaw frozen corn kernels, place them in a colander in the sink. While you're prepping the other ingredients, run warm water over corn until thawed.

Classic Hummus

1 ½ cups

prep: 10 minutes

2   (15.5-ounce) cans chickpeas
    (garbanzo beans), undrained

2   cloves garlic
2½ tablespoons tahini (see tip)
¼   cup lemon juice

1 Drain chickpeas, reserving ¼ cup liquid; set aside.

2 Process garlic in a food processor until minced. Add chickpeas, reserved ¼ cup liquid, the tahini, and lemon juice; process 3 minutes or until smooth, scraping down sides occasionally.

3 Transfer to a serving bowl. Serve immediately, or cover and chill. Serve with pita bread, pita chips, or fresh vegetables.

Flavor of Hummus

Hummus is typically served as a dip with wedges of pita bread or as a sandwich spread. It gets its distinctive flavor from tahini (sesame seed paste). Look for tahini in larger supermarkets or in Middle Eastern food stores.

Festive Cranberry-Cream Cheese Spread

6 to 8 appetizer servings

prep: 5 minutes

1   (8-ounce) package cream cheese
1   (12-ounce) container cranberry-
      raspberry crushed fruit for
      chicken
2   tablespoons amaretto (optional)

2   tablespoons chopped pecans

1 Place cream cheese on a serving plate. Combine crushed fruit and, if desired, amaretto; spoon over cream cheese.

2 Spread pecans in a pie plate; micro-wave, uncovered, at HIGH 1 to 2 minutes or until lightly toasted, stirring once. Sprinkle pecans over crushed fruit mixture. Serve immediately with crackers.

❝This appetizer is just the thing to bring out when unex-pected guests drop by. Chances are you'll have cream cheese and pecans on hand. So stock up on the fruit mixture and you're ready for anyone—and don't forget the crackers.❞

Grab 'n' Go Gorp

8 cups

prep: 5 minutes

2　cups crispy wheat cereal squares
2　cups mixed nuts
1　cup dried cherries
1　cup sweetened dried cranberries
1　cup dried blueberries
1　cup semisweet chocolate chips

1 Combine all ingredients; store in an airtight container.

Gorp is often used by athletes as an energy booster. The acronym is debated as standing for either 'good old raisins and peanuts,' or 'granola, oats, raisins, and peanuts.' Go ahead and dig into our variation of this merry mix of dried berries, chocolate, and nuts! It's high in fiber, vitamins, and protein, and is perfect for an after-school snack.

Spicy Cashews

3 cups

prep: 5 minutes   cook: 5 minutes

¼ cup butter
¼ cup vegetable oil
2 (7-ounce) jars dry-roasted cashews

½ teaspoon salt
½ teaspoon chili powder
¼ to ½ teaspoon ground red pepper

1 Melt butter with oil in a large skillet over medium heat; add cashews, and cook 3 to 5 minutes or until browned, stirring often. Remove cashews, and drain on paper towels; place cashews in a bowl.

2 Combine salt, chili powder, and ground red pepper in a small bowl. Sprinkle over warm cashews, tossing to coat.

Give your party a lively start with the spicy, bold flavor of these cashews. These small bites elevate the ordinary nut to extraordinary.

No-Chop Antipasto Tray

18 appetizer servings

prep: 8 minutes   cook: 6 minutes

1   (9-ounce) package refrigerated
      spinach tortellini
1   (12-ounce) jar peperoncini,
      undrained

1   (16-ounce) package fresh broccoli
      florets
1   (16-ounce) package fresh baby
      carrots
1   (14-ounce) can quartered artichoke
      hearts, drained
1   (8.5-ounce) package sliced
      pepperoni

2   tablespoons Dijon mustard
1   tablespoon olive oil

1 Cook tortellini according to package
directions; drain. Drain peperoncini,
reserving 3 tablespoons liquid.

2 Arrange tortellini, peperoncini, broccoli, and next 3 ingredients on a
large platter.

3 Combine reserved pepper liquid, the
mustard, and olive oil; stir well.
Drizzle mustard mixture over antipasto;
serve immediately, or cover and chill.

TIME-SAVIN' TIP

Watched pot won't boil? Place your saucepan over
high heat, and cover it. This causes a quicker buildup
of steam and pressure, resulting in a faster boil.

Blue Cheese Bites

4 dozen

prep: 15 minutes   chill: 2 hours   cook: 12 minutes

2   (4-ounce) packages crumbled blue
      cheese
½   cup butter, softened
1⅓   cups all-purpose flour
⅓   cup poppy seeds
¼   teaspoon ground red pepper

Walnut or pecan halves (optional)

1 Beat cheese and butter at medium speed of an electric beater until creamy. Add flour, poppy seeds, and red pepper; beat until blended.

2 Divide dough in half; shape each portion into an 8" log. Wrap in wax paper, and chill 2 hours or until firm.

3 Preheat the oven to 350°. Cut each log into ¼" slices; place on un-greased baking sheets. Press a walnut or pecan half in each slice, if desired. Bake at 350° for 10 to 12 minutes or until golden. Cool 1 minute on pans; remove to wire racks to cool completely.

TIME-SAVIN' TIP

The cheese logs can be chilled overnight and sliced and baked the next day. You can also vary the preparation by omitting the chilling time and rolling the dough to ¼" thickness. Using a 2" biscuit cutter or shaped cookie cutter, cut dough into rounds, and bake as directed.

Smoked Nachos

6 to 8 servings

prep: 10 minutes   cook: 15 minutes

1   (9-ounce) package tortilla chips
3   cups (12 ounces) shredded
      Cheddar-Jack-American cheese
      blend
½   cup sliced fresh or canned jalapeño
      peppers

1 Preheat the grill to low heat (under 300°). Spread chips in a lightly greased aluminum foil-lined 9" x 13" pan; sprinkle with cheese and jalapeños.

2 Place pan on grill rack, and grill, covered, 15 minutes or until cheese melts.

"These nachos are super easy, and the smoky flavor makes 'em a hands-down favorite. Plus, there's no cleanup! Serve 'em straight from the pan at your next cookout."

Hot Rye Rounds

about 3 dozen

prep: 14 minutes   cook: 10 minutes

4   bacon slices, cooked and crumbled
1   cup (4 ounces) shredded Swiss
        cheese
1   (4½-ounce) can chopped ripe olives
¼   cup mayonnaise
3   green onions, chopped
1   teaspoon Worcestershire sauce
½   teaspoon salt
Cocktail rye bread

1 Preheat the oven to 375°. Combine first 7 ingredients in a small bowl. Spread 1½ teaspoons cheese mixture onto each bread slice.

2 Arrange slices on ungreased baking sheets. Bake at 375° for 10 minutes or until lightly browned. Serve warm.

TIME-SAVIN' TIP

These pint-size ryes are a favorite finger food for parties. And they're easy to prepare ahead. Simply make the topping up to a day ahead, and refrigerate it. Top bread slices with the spread just before baking.

Pizza Snacks

8 snacks

prep: 10 minutes   cook: 12 minutes

1   (8-ounce) can refrigerated crescent
      rolls

1   (6-ounce) package pepperoni slices
2   (1-ounce) mozzarella cheese sticks,
      cut into fourths
1   teaspoon dried Italian seasoning
¼   teaspoon garlic salt

1 Preheat the oven to 375°. Separate rolls into 8 triangles, and place on a baking sheet.

2 Place 2 pepperoni slices on each triangle; place 1 piece of cheese at wide end of triangle. Sprinkle with Italian seasoning. Roll up, starting at wide end, and sprinkle with garlic salt.

3 Bake at 375° for 10 to 12 minutes or until golden.

❝These tasty rollups are a delicious snack for kids of any age. Let 'em lend a helping hand— they're ooh-so-easy to do!❞

Artichoke-Parmesan Crostini

44 appetizers

prep: 15 minutes   cook: 7 minutes per batch

1   (12-ounce) jar marinated artichoke hearts, drained and chopped
1   (4.5-ounce) can chopped green chilies, drained
1   cup shredded Parmesan cheese
1   cup mayonnaise
¼   cup finely chopped red bell pepper
2   cloves garlic, minced
44   baguette slices, lightly toasted (see tip)

1 Preheat the oven to 450°. Stir together first 6 ingredients. Spread 1 tablespoon artichoke mixture on each baguette slice, and place on ungreased baking sheets.

2 Bake at 450° for 6 to 7 minutes or until golden and bubbly. Serve hot.

TIME-SAVIN' TIP

For ease, buy toasted baguette slices from the grocery store bakery or substitute bagel chips or melba toast rounds for baguette slices.

Bring out your kitchen shears to chop artichoke hearts quickly.

Greek Olive Cups

30 appetizers

prep: 10 minutes   cook: 15 minutes

1   cup (4 ounces) shredded Cheddar
       cheese
½   cup chopped pimiento-stuffed
       olives
½   cup kalamata olives, pitted and
       chopped
⅓   cup chopped pecans, toasted
⅓   cup pine nuts, toasted
2   tablespoons mayonnaise
2   (2.1-ounce) packages frozen mini
       phyllo shells

1 Preheat the oven to 375°. Stir together first 6 ingredients. Remove phyllo shells from package, leaving them in trays.

2 Spoon 1 heaping teaspoon olive mixture into each pastry shell; remove from trays, and place cups on baking sheets.

3 Bake at 375° for 12 to 15 minutes or until thoroughly heated. Serve immediately.

TIME-SAVIN' TIP

After filling cups in trays, place trays in resealable plastic freezer bags, and freeze up to 1 month. Remove cups from trays, and place on a baking sheet. Let cups stand 10 minutes before baking. Bake as directed in recipe.

Tomato-Basil Squares

16 appetizers

prep: 10 minutes   cook: 20 minutes

1   (10-ounce) can refrigerated pizza
        crust
2   cups (8 ounces) shredded
        mozzarella cheese, divided
4   plum tomatoes, thinly sliced

⅔   cup mayonnaise
¼   cup grated Parmesan cheese
2   teaspoons dried basil
1   clove garlic, pressed

1 Preheat the oven to 375°. Unroll pizza crust, and press into a 10" x 15" rimmed baking sheet; sprinkle with 1 cup mozzarella cheese. Arrange tomato slices over cheese.

2 Combine remaining 1 cup mozzarella cheese, the mayonnaise, and remaining 3 ingredients; stir well. Spread cheese mixture over tomato slices. Bake at 375° for 20 minutes or until golden. Cut into 16 rectangles.

"Looking for an easy appetizer? Then try my cheesy tomato squares. Their pizza-like flavor really delivers!"

Sweet 'n' Savory Pizza

(pictured on page 4)

8 servings

prep: 10 minutes   cook: 5 minutes

8	ounces Brie
2	tablespoons butter
2	pears, peeled, cored, and thinly sliced
½	teaspoon ground cinnamon
1	(14-ounce) package prebaked Italian pizza bread shell
2	teaspoons olive oil
½	cup chopped pecans
4	tablespoons light brown sugar

1 Remove and discard rind from cheese. Cut cheese into cubes; set aside.

2 Melt butter in a large skillet over medium heat. Add pears, and sauté 3 minutes or until tender; sprinkle with cinnamon.

3 Preheat the oven to 500°. Place bread shell on a large pizza pan or baking sheet. Brush shell with olive oil, and top with cheese cubes. Spread cooked pear mixture over cheese; sprinkle with pecans and brown sugar. Bake at 500° for 5 minutes or until heated thoroughly. Slice pizza into wedges; serve immediately.

❝No one will be able to resist a slice of this gooey pizza that's both sweet and savory with each bite. 'Ooh it's so good!!'❞

Mulled Cranberry Drink

10 cups

prep: 5 minutes   cook: 10 minutes

1   (48-ounce) bottle cranberry juice
       drink
3   cups apple juice
3   cups orange juice
½   cup maple syrup
1½   teaspoons ground cinnamon
¾   teaspoon ground cloves
¾   teaspoon ground nutmeg

1   orange, sliced

1 Bring first 7 ingredients to a boil in a Dutch oven. Remove from heat; ladle into individual mugs, or transfer to a slow cooker to keep warm.

2 Add orange slices just before serving. Garnish with cinnamon sticks, if desired.

Beverages 101

Mulled drinks are beverages such as fruit juice, wine, cider, or beer that are flavored by heating with herbs, citrus fruit, and sugar or spices, as done in this recipe. They're a favorite wintertime beverage because they taste so good and their rich aromas fill the air with comforting fragrances.

Raspberry Lemonade

about 6 cups

prep: 10 minutes

1   (16-ounce) jar maraschino cherries
      without stems
1   (14-ounce) package frozen
      raspberries, thawed
1¼ cups sugar
¾   cup lemon juice (about 5 lemons)
¼   cup lime juice (about 2 limes)

3   cups water

1 Process first 5 ingredients in a blender until smooth, stopping occasionally to scrape down sides.

2 Pour fruit mixture through a wire-mesh strainer into a pitcher, discarding solids. Stir in 3 cups water. Serve over ice.

Fruity Picks

Blackberry Lemonade: Substitute 1 (14-ounce) package frozen blackberries, thawed, for frozen raspberries. Proceed with recipe as directed. Makes 6 cups.

Cherry-Berry Lemonade: Substitute 1 (16-ounce) package frozen mixed berries, thawed, for frozen raspberries. Proceed with recipe as directed, using 2 cups water. Makes 5 cups.

Cherry-Berry Lemonade Pops: Pour Cherry-Berry Lemonade evenly into 14 (4-ounce) plastic pop molds. Insert plastic pop sticks, and freeze 4 hours or until firm. Makes 14 pops.

Frothy Orange Soda

3 cups

prep: 5 minutes

1 cup orange juice
1 cup vanilla ice cream

1 cup lemon-lime soft drink

1 Process orange juice and ice cream in a blender 1 minute or until smooth.

2 Add lemon-lime soft drink; stir well. Pour into glasses; serve immediately.

"Ahh! This refreshing soda will remind you of that popular orange-vanilla ice cream bar you loved as a kid. It's guaranteed to quench your thirst on hot summer days."

Peach Yogurt Refresher

4½ cups

prep: 5 minutes

3   cups plain yogurt
1   cup sliced fresh peaches
½   cup water
6   tablespoons sugar

1 Process all ingredients in a blender until smooth, stopping occasionally to scrape down sides. Serve over ice.

"This shakelike beverage is a healthy and tasty way to start your day. Fresh mango slices are a refreshing substitute for fresh peaches—use equal amounts."

Fancy Schmancy in a Wink

“*A special occasion dinner doesn't mean laboring in the kitchen all day. With these recipes, you'll have dinner in a wink—giving you more time with family and friends.***”**

Parmesan Grouper Fillets

6 servings

prep: 5 minutes   cook: 20 minutes

¾ cup freshly grated Parmesan cheese
½ cup butter, softened
3 tablespoons mayonnaise
2 green onions, chopped

6 (8-ounce) grouper or other mild
   whitefish fillets (1" thick)
¼ cup lemon juice
½ teaspoon salt
½ teaspoon pepper

1 Preheat the broiler. Combine first 4 ingredients in a small bowl.

2 Place fish on a lightly greased rack in a broiler pan. Drizzle with lemon juice; sprinkle with salt and pepper. Broil 5½" from heat 15 minutes or until fish flakes easily with a fork.

3 Spread cheese mixture on fish. Broil 4 to 5 more minutes or until lightly browned and bubbly.

Fishing Around

If you can't find grouper or would rather use another fish, try one of these white-flesh alternatives: sea bass, orange roughy, or mahimahi.

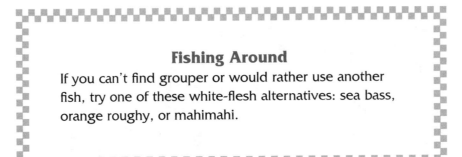

Lime-Baked Fish

6 servings

prep: 8 minutes   cook: 20 minutes

6	(6-ounce) halibut or other whitefish fillets (1" thick)
¾	teaspoon salt
½	teaspoon pepper
3	tablespoons lime juice
1	(8-ounce) container sour cream
1	tablespoon chopped fresh parsley or 1 teaspoon dried parsley
1	teaspoon grated lime rind

1 Preheat the oven to 400°. Place fish fillets in a greased 9" x 13" baking dish; sprinkle with salt and pepper.

2 Combine lime juice, sour cream, and parsley, stirring well; pour over fish. Sprinkle with lime rind.

3 Bake at 400° for 20 minutes or until fish flakes easily with a fork.

Add a Bit of Zest!
Grated lime rind adds pretty flecks of color and hints at the flavor of these fish fillets drenched with a lime juice-spiked sour cream sauce, so be sure to grate the lime before juicing it.

Maple-Glazed Salmon

2 servings

prep: 1 minute   cook: 10 minutes

1	tablespoon maple syrup
1	tablespoon hoisin sauce
1	teaspoon Dijon mustard
¼	teaspoon coarsely ground pepper
2	(6-ounce) salmon fillets (about 1" thick)

1 Preheat the broiler. Combine first 4 ingredients in a small bowl; stir with a whisk.

2 Place salmon, skin side down, on a broiler pan coated with nonstick cooking spray. Brush with maple mixture. Broil 5 minutes; brush with maple mixture. Broil 5 more minutes or until fish flakes easily with a fork, brushing with maple mixture.

TIME-SAVIN' TIP

Keep a package of individually wrapped salmon fillets in your freezer to pull out whenever you need them— this eliminates the extra trip to the fish market. Just thaw the fillets in the refrigerator overnight or in the microwave according to package directions. You can find them in the freezer section of your supermarket or warehouse grocery.

Zesty Fettuccine and Shrimp

2 to 4 servings

prep: 5 minutes   cook: 12 minutes

8   ounces dried fettuccine, uncooked

1   tablespoon olive oil
2   teaspoons blackening seasoning
¾   pound peeled, deveined large fresh
         shrimp (see tip)
2   tablespoons lemon juice
1   (14½-ounce) can diced tomatoes
         with roasted garlic, drained
¼   teaspoon pepper

1 Cook pasta according to package directions; drain and keep warm.

2 Meanwhile, heat oil in a large non-stick skillet over medium-high heat. Sprinkle blackening seasoning evenly over shrimp. Add shrimp to skillet; cook 2 minutes on each side or until shrimp turn pink. Stir in lemon juice. Add tomatoes and pepper; cook until thoroughly heated.

3 Spoon shrimp mixture over pasta, and serve immediately.

TIME-SAVIN' TIP

To save time, buy shrimp already peeled and deveined. But if you prefer to peel your own, you'll need 1 pound of unpeeled, large fresh shrimp.

Shrimp and Feta Scampi

(pictured on facing page)

4 servings

prep: 5 minutes   cook: 12 minutes

1   (8-ounce) package spaghetti

1½   pounds peeled, deveined large fresh
        shrimp (see tip)
1   (10-ounce) package frozen snow
        peas

4   green onions, sliced
⅓   cup olive oil vinaigrette
¼   teaspoon freshly ground pepper
½   cup crumbled feta cheese

1 Bring 2 quarts water to a boil in a large saucepan. Add pasta, and cook, uncovered, 9 minutes.

2 Add shrimp to pasta; cook, uncovered, 3 minutes or until shrimp turn pink. Place snow peas in a colander. Drain pasta and shrimp over snow peas.

3 Transfer mixture to a large serving bowl. Add onions, vinaigrette, and pepper; toss lightly. Sprinkle with crumbled feta cheese.

TIME-SAVIN' TIP

To save prep time, I call for peeled and deveined shrimp in my superfast recipes. If you want to start with unpeeled fresh shrimp, you'll need 2 pounds in order to end up with 1½ pounds of peeled shrimp. Also, by draining the pasta and shrimp over the snow peas, you've eliminated the need to thaw and cook the peas. The hot water from the pasta takes care of both!

Pepper-Beef Stir-Fry,
page 78

Focaccia Sandwich,
page 87

Wine-Glazed Chicken

(pictured on facing page)

4 servings

prep: 10 minutes   cook: 35 minutes

1   teaspoon salt
½   teaspoon ground nutmeg
8   chicken legs

¼   cup butter

1⅓   cups dry white wine or sparkling
        white grape juice
1   cup sliced fresh mushrooms
1   red bell pepper, thinly sliced
3   green onions, chopped

2   tablespoons chicken broth
4   teaspoons cornstarch
Warm cooked rice

1 Sprinkle salt and ground nutmeg over chicken.

2 Melt butter in a medium skillet over medium heat; add chicken. Cook 10 minutes or until golden, turning often.

3 Stir in wine and next 3 ingredients; bring to a boil over medium heat. Reduce heat to medium-low; cover and simmer 20 minutes or until chicken is done. Remove chicken from skillet, and keep warm.

4 Whisk together broth and cornstarch until smooth; add to drippings in skillet. Cook over medium heat, stirring constantly, 1 minute or until thickened. Serve drumsticks over rice; spoon glaze over chicken.

"These ordinary drumsticks get dressed up in this fancy schmancy recipe! Feel free to substitute chicken thighs or wings for the legs if you prefer."

Sautéed Chicken in Lemon Sauce

6 servings

prep: 12 minutes   cook: 22 minutes

6   skinned and boned chicken breasts
½   teaspoon salt, divided
¼   teaspoon pepper, divided

¼   cup butter

2   tablespoons dry vermouth or
        2 tablespoons chicken broth
2   teaspoons grated lemon rind (see
        tip on page 33)
2   tablespoons lemon juice
¾   cup whipping cream
½   cup chicken broth

½   cup grated Parmesan cheese, divided
¼   cup chopped fresh parsley or 1½
        tablespoons dried parsley

1 Place chicken between 2 sheets of heavy-duty plastic wrap, and flatten to ½" thickness, using a meat mallet or rolling pin. Sprinkle with ¼ teaspoon salt and ⅛ teaspoon pepper.

2 Melt butter in a large skillet over medium-high heat. Add chicken; cook 3 to 5 minutes on each side or until golden. Remove chicken from skillet. Set aside, and keep warm. Wipe skillet with paper towels.

3 Add vermouth, lemon rind, and lemon juice to skillet; cook 1 minute, stirring to loosen particles from bottom of skillet. Stir in whipping cream and chicken broth. Bring to a boil; reduce heat, and simmer, uncovered, 5 to 6 minutes, stirring occasionally.

4 Stir in ¼ cup Parmesan cheese, remaining ¼ teaspoon salt, and remaining ⅛ teaspoon pepper; simmer 1 minute, stirring constantly. Pour sauce over chicken; sprinkle with remaining ¼ cup Parmesan cheese and the parsley.

TIME-SAVIN' TIP

You can grate the rind of lemons, oranges, or limes ahead and freeze. Just wrap the grated rind tightly in plastic wrap, and freeze. It's ready when you are. No need to thaw!

Grilled Jerk Chicken

(pictured on page 2)

4 servings

prep: 3 minutes   cook: 12 minutes

1   tablespoon lime juice
1½   teaspoons vegetable oil
4   (4-ounce) skinned and boned
        chicken breasts
1   tablespoon jerk seasoning

1 Spray cold grill rack with nonstick cooking spray; preheat the grill to medium-high heat (350° to 400°). Combine lime juice and oil in a small bowl; brush over both sides of chicken. Sprinkle chicken evenly with seasoning.

2 Place chicken on heated grill rack; grill, covered, 5 to 6 minutes on each side or until done.

"Tame the heat of this chicken by serving it with a fruit salsa. You can make your own or find it in larger supermarkets. It's a great combination."

Feta Chicken with Oregano

4 servings

prep: 10 minutes   marinate: 30 minutes   cook: 15 minutes

1   (8-ounce) container plain yogurt
2   large cloves garlic, minced
1   tablespoon chopped fresh oregano
        or 1 teaspoon dried oregano
½   teaspoon freshly ground pepper
4   skinned and boned chicken breasts

¾   cup crumbled feta cheese

1 Combine first 4 ingredients in a large bowl. Add chicken; turn to coat. Cover and marinate in refrigerator 30 minutes, turning after 15 minutes.

2 Preheat the broiler. Remove chicken from marinade, reserving marinade. Place chicken on a lightly greased rack in a broiler pan; brush with remaining marinade. Broil 5½" from heat 8 to 10 minutes. Turn chicken; sprinkle evenly with feta cheese. Broil 4 to 5 more minutes or until chicken is done and golden. Serve immediately.

"This Greek-inspired entrée is tenderized by a marinade of plain yogurt that's laced with garlic and oregano. Because of its intense flavor, I recommend using fresh oregano if it's available. Topping the chicken with a sprinkle of feta cheese carries out the Mediterranean theme of this simple chicken dish."

Summer Lime Chicken

4 servings

prep: 8 minutes   chill: 1 hour   cook: 20 minutes

⅓   cup olive oil
¼   cup lime juice
3   cloves garlic, halved
3   tablespoons minced fresh cilantro
½   teaspoon salt
½   teaspoon pepper

4   skinned and boned chicken breasts

1 Combine first 6 ingredients in a small bowl; stir with a whisk. Reserve 2 tablespoons marinade for basting.

2 Place chicken in a large resealable plastic freezer bag. Pour remaining marinade over chicken, and seal. Marinate in refrigerator 1 hour, turning occasionally.

3 Preheat the grill to medium-high heat (350° to 400°). Remove chicken from marinade; discard marinade. Grill, covered, about 20 minutes or until done, turning once and basting occasionally with the reserved 2 tablespoons marinade.

"Generous amounts of lime juice, garlic, and cilantro create a marinade that only needs to mingle with the chicken for an hour to infuse it with great flavor."

Chicken with Sun-Dried Tomatoes

4 servings

prep: 10 minutes   cook: 17 minutes

1½ tablespoons butter
4   skinned and boned chicken breasts,
        cut into strips (see tip)

1   large shallot, minced (see tip)
1   tablespoon Dijon mustard
1   cup heavy whipping cream
2   tablespoons dry white wine or
        chicken broth
1½ tablespoons dried tarragon
1   (3-ounce) package sun-dried
        tomatoes, hydrated and chopped

1 Melt butter in a large skillet over medium-high heat. Add chicken, and sauté 8 minutes or until lightly browned on both sides. Remove chicken from skillet, and set aside.

2 Add shallot to skillet, and sauté 1 minute. Add mustard and remaining 4 ingredients to skillet. Cook over medium heat until sauce thickens slightly, stirring occasionally.

3 Return chicken to skillet, and simmer until thoroughly heated. Serve with rice or pasta.

Handy Substitutions
You can use chicken tenders instead of chicken breasts in this dish that's richly flavored with sun-dried tomatoes, white wine, and tarragon. And if shallots aren't available, substitute 2 tablespoons of minced onion plus 1 tablespoon of minced garlic.

Red Curry Chicken

4 servings

prep: 5 minutes   cook: 16 minutes

1   (16-ounce) package frozen broccoli,
      red peppers, onions, and
      mushrooms

1   tablespoon vegetable oil
1   (6-ounce) package grilled chicken
      breast strips
1   (13.5-ounce) can coconut milk
2   teaspoons red curry paste (see note)
½   teaspoon salt

2   tablespoons thinly sliced fresh basil
      or 2 teaspoons dried basil

1 Place vegetables in a microwave-safe bowl; cover with plastic wrap, and vent. Microwave at HIGH 4 minutes; drain and set aside.

2 Meanwhile, heat oil in a large non-stick skillet over medium-high heat. Add chicken, and sauté 1 minute. Add coconut milk; bring to a boil. Stir in red curry paste and salt. Cook 5 minutes over medium heat or just until sauce begins to thicken, stirring frequently.

3 Add vegetable mixture to chicken mixture. Bring to a boil; cook 4 minutes or until slightly thickened. Stir in basil. Serve over warm cooked rice, and sprinkle with chopped peanuts, if desired.

Note: Find red curry paste in the ethnic food aisle of larger supermarkets.

Dinner Plan
Make the most of your time in the kitchen. While your rice cooks, slice the basil and chop some peanuts to give this dish extra flavor; then cook the vegetables in the microwave. Meanwhile, begin cooking the chicken.

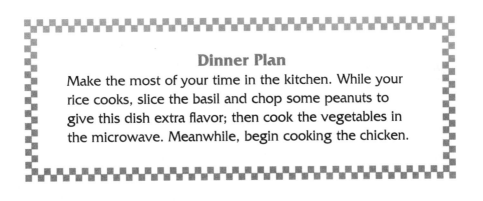

Chicken Livers Stroganoff

2 servings

prep: 8 minutes   cook: 30 minutes

1	tablespoon vegetable oil
1	medium onion, chopped
1	(8-ounce) package sliced fresh mushrooms
½	pound chicken livers
1	tablespoon all-purpose flour
6	tablespoons chicken broth
¼	cup dry white wine
2	tablespoons chili sauce or ketchup
¼	teaspoon salt
¼	teaspoon pepper
½	cup sour cream

1 Heat oil in a large skillet over medium-high heat. Add onion, and sauté 6 minutes or until golden. Add mushrooms, and sauté 5 minutes. Add chicken livers; sauté 5 minutes.

2 Combine flour and next 5 ingredients, stirring until smooth. Stir flour mixture into liver mixture. Bring to a boil; cover, reduce heat, and simmer 10 minutes or until livers are done.

3 Stir in sour cream. Cook just until thoroughly heated. Serve over brown rice, if desired.

Cut Cost, Not Flavor

Enjoy all the creamy goodness and richness of traditional stroganoff at a fraction of the cost by using chicken livers instead of beef. You won't hear anyone asking "Where's the beef?".

Peppercorn Pork Scaloppine

4 servings

prep: 15 minutes   cook: 10 minutes

1   pound pork tenderloin or boneless
        pork loin
¼   teaspoon salt
¼   teaspoon freshly ground black
        pepper

2   tablespoons olive oil
2   tablespoons butter
1   clove garlic, crushed

2   tablespoons pickled green
        peppercorns, drained, or 2
        tablespoons capers, drained
        (see tip)
1   teaspoon lemon juice

1 Cut pork crosswise into 8 slices. Place pork between 2 sheets of heavy-duty plastic wrap, and flatten to ¼" thickness, using a meat mallet or rolling pin. Sprinkle pork evenly with salt and pepper.

2 Heat 1 tablespoon olive oil and 1 tablespoon butter in a large nonstick skillet over medium-high heat until hot. Add garlic and half of pork; cook 2 minutes on each side. Transfer pork to a platter, and keep warm. Repeat process with remaining oil, butter, and pork; transfer to platter.

3 Discard garlic. Add peppercorns and lemon juice to skillet; cook 30 seconds. Pour sauce over pork, and serve immediately.

Pickled Peppercorns

Pounding the pork loin tenderizes the meat and allows it to cook faster. A bit of tangy green peppercorn sauce flavors these pork medallions nicely. Look for pickled green peppercorns in the condiment aisle of your supermarket.

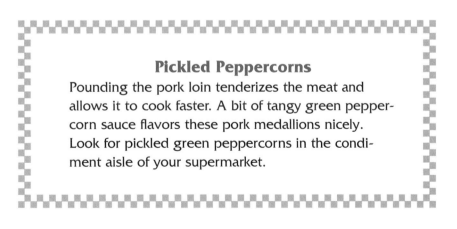

Smoked Pork Chops with Jalapeño-Cherry Sauce

6 servings

prep: 10 minutes   cook: 12 minutes

6   (1" thick) boneless smoked pork
      chops

1   (14-ounce) can dark, sweet pitted
      cherries
1   cup hot jalapeño jelly
½   teaspoon ground coriander
      (optional)

1 Preheat the grill to medium-high heat (350° to 400°). Place pork chops on grill rack; grill, covered, 5 to 6 minutes on each side or until done. Transfer to a serving platter.

2 Bring cherries, jelly, and, if desired, coriander to a boil in a saucepan, stirring constantly. Pour over pork chops.

"The simple, spicy-sweet sauce really enhances the smoky pork—with just three ingredients!"

Spaghetti Carbonara

4 to 6 servings

prep: 10 minutes   cook: 15 minutes

12   ounces uncooked spaghetti

8   bacon slices, cut into 1" pieces
1   small onion, chopped
1   clove garlic, minced

2   cups half-and-half
½   cup freshly grated Parmesan cheese
1   large egg, lightly beaten
¼   teaspoon salt
½   teaspoon pepper
2   tablespoons chopped fresh parsley

1 Cook spaghetti according to package directions; drain and keep warm.

2 Meanwhile, cook bacon, onion, and garlic in a large nonstick skillet over medium-high heat until bacon is crisp.

3 Whisk together half-and-half, ¼ cup Parmesan cheese, and the next 3 ingredients; toss in spaghetti. Add spaghetti mixture to bacon mixture in skillet; cook over medium-low heat 5 minutes, stirring occasionally. Sprinkle each serving evenly with remaining cheese and the parsley.

Safety First

Traditionally, the ingredients for this dish are stirred into hot pasta and served. In this recipe, you toss the raw egg mixture with spaghetti and reheat it in a skillet to follow food safety guidelines.

Lamb Chops Stilton

4 servings

prep: 5 minutes   cook: 11 minutes

8   (1" thick) lamb loin chops
8   teaspoons Dijon mustard, divided

6   ounces Stilton or other blue cheese,
     crumbled

"No one would ever guess that this 3-ingredient dish is such a snap to prepare! It tastes like something from a five-star restaurant. Bon appetit!"

1 Preheat the broiler. Place lamb chops on a lightly greased rack in a broiler pan. Brush top of each chop with ½ teaspoon mustard.

2 Broil chops 5 minutes. Turn chops, and brush each with ½ teaspoon mustard. Broil 5 more minutes.

3 Sprinkle chops evenly with crumbled cheese, and broil 1 minute or until cheese melts. Serve immediately.

Hazelnut and Mustard Lamb Chops

2 servings

prep: 14 minutes   cook: 25 minutes

¼   cup coarse-grained Dijon mustard
2   tablespoons dry white wine
½   cup ground hazelnuts
¼   cup soft breadcrumbs (homemade)
1½   teaspoons minced garlic

4   (2- to 3-ounce) lamb loin chops
1   teaspoon freshly ground pepper
2   tablespoons olive oil

1½   tablespoons butter, melted

1 Preheat the oven to 375°. Stir together mustard and wine in a shallow dish; set aside. Stir together hazelnuts, breadcrumbs, and garlic in a shallow dish; set aside.

2 Sprinkle lamb chops with pepper. Heat oil in a large skillet over medium-high heat until hot. Add chops; cook 2 minutes on each side or until browned. Remove chops from skillet, and dip in mustard mixture. Then dredge all sides in breadcrumb mixture, pressing well.

3 Place chops in a lightly greased shallow roasting pan; drizzle with melted butter. Bake at 375° for 20 minutes or to desired degree of doneness.

On the "Lamb"

When shopping, look for lamb with bright pink color, pink bones, and white fat. If you find dark red meat and bones, then the meat is usually older. With the exception of ground, all other cuts of lamb can be refrigerated 2 days or frozen up to 9 months. Refrigerate ground lamb for only 1 day and freeze up to 4 months.

Steaks with Caramel-Brandy Sauce

4 servings

prep: 5 minutes   cook: 12 minutes

4	(6-ounce) beef tenderloin fillets
1	teaspoon salt
1	teaspoon pepper
3	tablespoons butter, divided
3	tablespoons brandy
1	tablespoon light brown sugar
¼	cup whipping cream

1 Sprinkle steaks evenly with salt and pepper. Melt 1 tablespoon butter in a medium skillet over medium-high heat. Add steaks; cook 3 minutes on each side or to desired degree of doneness. Remove steaks from skillet, and keep warm.

2 Add brandy to skillet, stirring to loosen particles from bottom of skillet. Add remaining 2 tablespoons butter and the sugar; cook, stirring constantly, until sugar dissolves and browns.

3 Remove skillet from heat; whisk in cream until blended. Return to heat, and bring to a boil; cook, stirring constantly, 1 minute or until thickened. Serve immediately over steaks.

As You Like It

This recipe cooks the steaks to medium-rare doneness. For more well-done steaks, lower the temperature and increase cooking time.

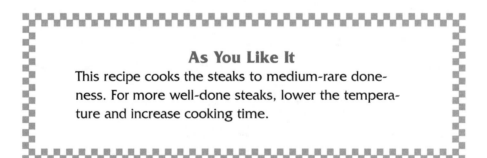

Grecian Skillet Rib Eyes

2 to 4 servings

prep: 5 minutes   cook: 15 minutes

1½ teaspoons garlic powder
1½ teaspoons dried oregano, crushed
½   teaspoon salt
½   teaspoon pepper
2   (1" thick) rib-eye steaks (about
     2 pounds)

1   tablespoon olive oil
1   tablespoon lemon juice
¼   cup crumbled feta cheese
2   tablespoons chopped kalamata or
     ripe olives

1 Combine first 4 ingredients; rub onto all sides of steaks.

2 Heat oil in a large nonstick skillet over medium heat until hot. Add steaks, and cook 10 to 14 minutes or to desired degree of doneness, turning once. Remove to a serving platter. Sprinkle with lemon juice; top with cheese and olives.

Good Grades

The grade of beef that you buy will determine how good your steak is. The USDA inspects all beef products to determine the "grade." The most commonly found grades in retail grocery stores are select, choice, and prime.

Select is the least expensive grade and contains the least marbling. Marbling is flecks of whitish fat that runs throughout meat, especially beef. It makes meat more flavorful, tender, and juicy.

Choice is the most popular grade. It has less marbling than prime but enough fat to still be tender when cooked with dry heat.

Prime is the highest grade—and the most expensive beef. You'll find it's well-marbled.

Fettuccine with Blue Cheese-Artichoke Sauce

3 to 4 servings

prep: 5 minutes   cook: 10 minutes

1   (9-ounce) package refrigerated
      fettuccine

1   (14-ounce) can quartered artichoke
      hearts, drained
1   cup sliced fresh mushrooms
1   (10-ounce) container refrigerated
      Alfredo sauce

2   tablespoons crumbled blue cheese

1 Cook pasta according to package directions; drain and keep warm.

2 Meanwhile, cook artichokes and mushrooms in a large nonstick skillet coated with nonstick cooking spray over medium-high heat 3 to 4 minutes or until mushrooms are tender. Add Alfredo sauce to artichoke mixture; cook until thoroughly heated.

3 Place pasta in a large bowl. Pour sauce mixture over pasta; toss to combine. Sprinkle with cheese.

TIME-SAVIN' TIP

Convenience products bring this creamy, cheesy meal to the table in 15 minutes! Purchase presliced mushrooms to make prep no more trouble than opening up packages!

Ravioli with Roasted Red Pepper Cream

4 servings

prep: 5 minutes   cook: 15 minutes

1	(24-ounce) package frozen cheese ravioli
2½	quarts boiling water
1	(7-ounce) jar roasted sweet red peppers, drained, seeded, and cut into strips
½	cup dry white wine
1	cup whipping cream
¾	cup freshly grated Parmesan cheese

1 Cook ravioli in boiling water 5 minutes or until tender. Drain; set aside, and keep warm.

2 Meanwhile, combine peppers and wine in a saucepan. Bring to a boil; reduce heat, and simmer, uncovered, 5 minutes or until reduced to 2 tablespoons. Stir in whipping cream. Bring to a boil; reduce heat, and simmer, uncovered, 3 to 5 minutes or until slightly thickened, stirring often. Add Parmesan cheese, and cook, stirring constantly, until cheese melts.

3 Divide ravioli among 4 individual serving bowls. Spoon sauce evenly over pasta. Serve immediately.

❝If you're looking for a simple, yet rich-tasting dish that tastes like it took hours, this 15-minute miracle fits the bill. A salad and breadsticks are all you need to complete the meal!❞

Rotini with Artichokes and Sun-Dried Tomatoes

6 to 8 servings

prep: 10 minutes   cook: 10 minutes

1   (16-ounce) package rotini pasta

2   (6-ounce) jars marinated artichoke
      hearts, drained and quartered

¾   to 1 cup Italian dressing

1   (6-ounce) can pitted black olives,
      drained and quartered

1   (7-ounce) jar marinated sun-dried
      tomatoes in oil, drained and
      chopped

10   fresh basil leaves, thinly shredded

1   large red bell pepper, diced

½   teaspoon salt

1 Cook pasta according to package directions. Drain pasta; rinse and place in a large bowl.

2 Combine artichoke hearts, ¾ cup dressing, and the next 5 ingredients. Toss with pasta, adding additional dressing, if desired.

If you have extra time, try your hand at preparing homemade dressing instead of buying ready-made Italian dressing. Use equal parts balsamic vinegar and olive oil, and add your favorite herbs and spices.

White Tie Pasta

4 to 6 servings

prep: 6 minutes   cook: 15 minutes

8   ounces bow tie pasta, uncooked

8   bacon slices, cut into pieces

1   (14-ounce) can quartered artichoke
      hearts, drained
1   (8-ounce) package sliced fresh
      mushrooms
1   cup sliced green onions

1   (10-ounce) container refrigerated
      Alfredo sauce
2   tablespoons pine nuts, toasted
      (see tip)
¾   teaspoon freshly ground pepper
1   cup shredded Parmesan cheese

1 Cook pasta according to package directions; drain and keep warm.

2 Meanwhile, cook bacon in a large nonstick skillet over medium-high heat until crisp; remove bacon, reserving drippings in skillet.

3 Add artichokes, mushrooms, and green onions to skillet; cook 5 minutes over medium-high heat until tender. Stir in bacon.

4 Combine pasta, Alfredo sauce, artichoke mixture, pine nuts, and pepper in a large bowl. Sprinkle each serving with Parmesan cheese.

Aw, Nuts!
Take the time to toast the pine nuts for this recipe. Toasting helps them stay crisp and enhances their rich, delicate flavor. To toast pine nuts, simply place them in a dry skillet over medium heat, and cook 2 to 3 minutes, stirring often.

Mushroom 'n' Pesto Pizza

6 servings

prep: 10 minutes   cook: 25 minutes

1   (8-ounce) package sliced fresh
      button mushrooms
½   large onion, sliced
½   teaspoon salt
½   teaspoon pepper
1   tablespoon balsamic vinegar

2   tablespoons yellow cornmeal
1   (10-ounce) can refrigerated pizza
      crust

¼   cup basil pesto
6   fresh mozzarella cheese slices
      (6 ounces)
5   plum tomatoes, chopped
Shredded Parmesan cheese

1 Sauté first 4 ingredients in a large skillet coated with nonstick cooking spray over medium-high heat 5 minutes or until onion is tender. Add balsamic vinegar; cook 2 minutes or until liquid is evaporated. Set aside.

2 Meanwhile, preheat the oven to 425°. Sprinkle cornmeal over an ungreased 10" x 15" rimmed baking pan; spread out pizza crust. Bake on bottom oven rack at 425° for 5 minutes.

3 Spread pesto over pizza crust, leaving a 1" border. Sprinkle with mushroom mixture. Top with mozzarella cheese and tomatoes. Sprinkle with Parmesan cheese.

4 Bake at 425° on bottom oven rack for 18 minutes or until edges are golden brown and cheese is melted.

66Refrigerated pizza crust gives you a head start. And for a more smoky flavor and meaty texture, use 2 large Portobello mushroom caps that have been sliced instead of the button mushrooms. Either way, you've got a winner!99

Snappy Weeknight Favorites

"Dinner's on the table in no time flat with these easy, speedy weeknight favorites."

Golden Catfish Fillets

6 servings

prep: 7 minutes   cook: 10 minutes

1   cup cornmeal
1¼   teaspoons garlic salt
¼   teaspoon ground red pepper
⅛   teaspoon black pepper

1   egg white
1   cup milk
6   (6-ounce) catfish fillets (½" thick)

Vegetable oil

1 Combine first 4 ingredients in a shallow dish; set aside.

2 Whisk together egg white and milk in a shallow dish. Dip fillets in egg mixture; dredge in cornmeal mixture.

3 Pour oil to a depth of ¼" into a large heavy skillet (do not use a nonstick skillet). Fry fillets in hot oil over medium-high heat 4 minutes on each side or until golden. Drain on paper towels.

"Red and black pepper add zip to this crispy, crunchy cornmeal coating. Pair this easy catfish dish with my Creole Hush Puppies (page 145)—they're the perfect Southern accompaniment."

Zesty Fish Po'Boys

4 servings

prep: 5 minutes   cook: 20 minutes

2   (11-ounce) packages frozen
     breaded fish fillets

1   cup mayonnaise
3   tablespoons lemon juice
1   tablespoon Creole mustard
1   tablespoon sweet pickle relish
½   teaspoon dried parsley
¼   teaspoon dried tarragon
½   teaspoon hot sauce

2   (12") French bread loaves
4   lettuce leaves

1 Bake fish fillets according to package directions. Set aside, and keep warm.

2 Meanwhile, stir together mayonnaise and next 6 ingredients.

3 Cut bread in half crosswise. Split each half lengthwise, and toast in the preheated oven. Spread mayonnaise mixture evenly over cut side of bread halves. Place lettuce and fish on bottom bread halves; top with remaining bread halves. Serve immediately.

TIME-SAVIN' TIP

For time-stretched nights, jump-start dinner with a package of frozen fish fillets, and dinner's on the table in 25 minutes. This sandwich spread does double-duty when you use it as a dressing and combine it with coleslaw mix. Now you have a complete supper in minutes.

Speedy Chicken Cacciatore

3 to 4 servings

prep: 3 minutes   cook: 12 minutes

1   tablespoon olive oil
1   (20-ounce) package frozen cooked
        diced chicken breast
1   medium-sized green bell pepper,
        cut into 1" pieces
1   small onion, cut into 1" pieces

1   (9-ounce) package refrigerated
        angel hair pasta

1   (15-ounce) can chunky Italian-style
        tomato sauce
⅔   cup water
¼   teaspoon black pepper

1 Heat olive oil in a large nonstick skillet over medium-high heat until hot. Add chicken, green pepper, and onion; sauté until chicken is browned and vegetables are crisp-tender.

2 While chicken cooks, cook pasta according to package directions. Drain and keep warm.

3 Stir tomato sauce, water, and black pepper into chicken mixture. Reduce heat, and simmer, uncovered, 5 minutes, stirring often. Place pasta on each of 4 plates; top each serving evenly with chicken mixture.

TIME-SAVIN' TIP

Frozen cooked chicken breasts and refrigerated pasta are what make this a speedy version of the Italian classic. Fresh pasta cooks in 1 to 3 minutes as compared to the 6 to 15 minutes it takes for dried pasta to cook. Put on the pot of water to boil for pasta as soon as you start this dish, and everything will be ready in no time!

Ranch Chicken Fettuccine

3 to 4 servings

prep: 10 minutes   cook: 14 minutes

2   tablespoons olive oil
1   (12-ounce) package fresh broccoli
        florets
1   medium-sized red bell pepper,
        diced
1   clove garlic, minced

1   (9-ounce) package refrigerated
        fettuccine

2   (6-ounce) packages grilled chicken
        breast strips
4   sun-dried tomato halves in oil,
        drained and chopped
2   teaspoons minced fresh rosemary or
        2 teaspoons dried rosemary

1   (8-ounce) bottle Ranch-style
        dressing
¼   cup grated Parmesan cheese

1 Heat oil in large skillet over medium-high heat. Add broccoli and bell pepper, and sauté 7 minutes or until crisp-tender; add garlic, and sauté 2 minutes.

2 While vegetables cook, prepare pasta according to package directions. Drain and keep warm.

3 Stir chicken and tomatoes into vegetable mixture; sprinkle with rosemary. Cook until thoroughly heated, stirring occasionally.

4 Toss together pasta, broccoli mixture, Ranch dressing, and cheese.

Dressing Up

Ranch-style dressing now comes in a variety of flavors. Try any of them to give this simple dish an additional boost of flavor. Bring pasta water to a boil as soon as you start the dish so everything gets done at the same time.

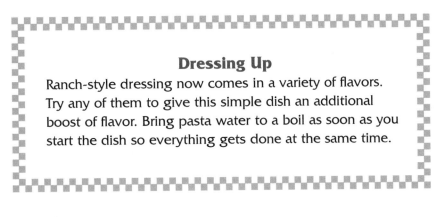

Chicken Reuben Casserole

4 servings

prep: 10 minutes   cook: 30 minutes

4   skinned and boned chicken breasts
½   teaspoon salt
¼   teaspoon pepper

1   (14.5-ounce) can sauerkraut, drained
8   deli corned beef slices
8   (1-ounce) Swiss cheese slices
1½   cups Thousand Island dressing

1   cup soft rye breadcrumbs
2   tablespoons butter, melted
1   tablespoon chopped fresh parsley

1 Preheat the oven to 350°. Sprinkle chicken with salt and pepper; place in a lightly greased 9" x 13" baking dish.

2 Layer chicken evenly with sauerkraut, corned beef, and Swiss cheese. Pour dressing over top.

3 Combine breadcrumbs, butter, and parsley; sprinkle over casserole. Bake, uncovered, at 350° for 30 minutes or until golden and bubbly.

"This easy-to-make casserole has the same tasty ingredients as the classic sandwich but presents them in a fresh, new way. See for yourself why it's one of my favorites!"

Cheesy Chicken Spaghetti Casserole

4 to 6 servings

prep: 4 minutes   cook: 25 minutes

8 ounces uncooked spaghetti
2 cups (8 ounces) shredded Cheddar cheese, divided
1 (26-ounce) jar spaghetti sauce
1 (20-ounce) package frozen cooked diced chicken breast, thawed (see tip)

1 Cook pasta according to package directions; drain well.

2 Preheat the oven to 350°. Combine pasta, 1 cup cheese, the sauce, and chicken in a large bowl; spoon into a lightly greased 9" x 13" baking dish. Sprinkle with remaining 1 cup cheese.

3 Bake, uncovered, at 350° for 15 minutes or until cheese melts.

" I use already cooked and diced chicken breast in this recipe to save even more time in the kitchen. But if you have chicken breasts already on hand, that's great, too. You'll need 3 cups of chopped cooked chicken. "

Skillet Chicken Divan

4 servings

prep: 5 minutes   cook: 17 minutes

1   family-size bag quick-cooking
    boil-in-bag rice

1   (9-ounce) package frozen diced
    cooked chicken breast
½   (16-ounce) package fresh broccoli
    florets
2   tablespoons water

1   (10¾-ounce) can cream of chicken
    and broccoli soup, undiluted
1   cup milk
½   cup (2 ounces) shredded sharp
    Cheddar cheese
½   teaspoon curry powder
¼   teaspoon salt
¼   teaspoon pepper

1 Cook rice according to package directions; drain and keep warm.

2 While rice cooks, coat a large non-stick skillet with nonstick cooking spray; place over medium-high heat until hot. Add chicken and broccoli; cook 6 minutes or until chicken is thawed and broccoli is crisp-tender, adding 2 tablespoons water, if necessary, to prevent sticking.

3 Combine soup and next 5 ingredients, stirring well. Add to broccoli mixture. Cook, uncovered, over medium-low heat 10 minutes, stirring occasionally. Serve over rice.

TIME-SAVIN' TIP

Products such as precooked chicken, precut broccoli, quick-cooking rice, and preshredded cheese really help cut the prep time in this recipe.
    A simple fruit salad is a great choice to round out this meal—you can even buy your fruit already cut.

Barbecued Chicken Pizza

4 servings

prep: 15 minutes   cook: 15 minutes

2   cups chopped cooked chicken
¾   cup barbecue sauce

1   (14-ounce) package prebaked Italian
       pizza bread shell
1   cup (4 ounces) shredded mozzarella
       cheese
¼   medium-sized red onion, thinly
       sliced
2   green onions, chopped

1 Preheat the oven to 450°. Combine chicken and barbecue sauce; let stand 15 minutes.

2 Place bread shell on a baking sheet. Spread chicken mixture over bread shell. Top with cheese and remaining ingredients. Bake at 450° for 15 minutes or until cheese melts.

"In the time it takes to have pizza delivered to your home, you can already have this tasty pizza on the table. Convenience products make it super quick!"

Turkey Parmesan

2 servings

prep: 5 minutes   cook: 5 minutes

½   pound turkey cutlets
¼   cup classic Italian-seasoned coating
       mix for chicken

1   tablespoon olive oil

½   cup tomato-basil pasta sauce
¼   cup shredded Parmesan cheese

1 Place cutlets between 2 sheets of heavy-duty plastic wrap, and flatten to ⅛" thickness, using a mallet or rolling pin. Coat both sides of cutlets with coating mix.

2 Heat olive oil in a large nonstick skillet over medium-high heat. Add cutlets; cook 2 minutes on each side or until lightly browned. Transfer to a serving platter; keep warm.

3 Place sauce in a microwave-safe dish; microwave at HIGH 1 minute or until heated. Spoon over cutlets; sprinkle with cheese.

TIME-SAVIN' TIP

Save prep time by purchasing preseasoned coating mix—all you need is in one convenient package. You can find this coating mix in the baking section of your supermarket.

Round out your meal with angel hair pasta and Italian bread—delizioso!

Cranberry Turkey Melts

4 servings

prep: 3 minutes   cook: 10 minutes

2   (6") prebaked Italian pizza bread
       shells
½   cup cranberry-orange sauce
½   pound thinly sliced cooked turkey
       breast, cut into strips
⅔   cup (2.6 ounces) shredded pepper
       Jack cheese

1 Preheat the oven to 450°. Place bread
      shells on ungreased baking sheets.
Spread bread shells with cranberry-
orange sauce. Arrange turkey strips over
sauce, and sprinkle with cheese.

2 Bake at 450° for 8 to 10 minutes or
      until cheese melts.

*"This is a wonderful idea for holiday leftovers! But
don't despair when the holidays are over—deli-style
turkey works just as great."*

Spicy Mustard Pork Chops

6 servings

prep: 10 minutes   cook: 6 minutes

½	teaspoon salt
½	teaspoon garlic powder
¼	teaspoon pepper
½	cup spicy brown mustard
6	(½" thick) boneless pork chops
1	cup all-purpose flour
¼	cup vegetable or canola oil

1 Combine first 3 ingredients. Spread mustard evenly on both sides of pork chops, and sprinkle with salt mixture.

2 Place flour in a shallow dish; dredge chops in flour.

3 Heat oil in a large skillet over medium-high heat. Cook pork chops 2 to 3 minutes on each side or until golden. Drain on paper towels, and serve immediately.

"If you have hearty eaters in your family, then consider this a 3-serving recipe, since they can probably eat 2 chops apiece!"

Salsa Pork Chops

4 servings

prep: 5 minutes   cook: 16 minutes

1   cup thick and chunky salsa (see tip)
1   (15-ounce) can crushed pineapple in juice, undrained
4   green onions, chopped

2   tablespoons vegetable oil
4   (5-ounce) center-cut pork loin chops, trimmed

1 Combine first 3 ingredients in a bowl; set aside.

2 Heat oil in a large nonstick skillet over medium-high heat until hot. Add pork chops, and cook 4 minutes on each side or until browned. Add salsa mixture to skillet; simmer, uncovered, 8 minutes or until pork is done, turning occasionally.

Heat It Up!
If you like your food with a kick, you're in control! Salsa comes in hot, medium, and mild varieties—we'll leave the choice up to you!

Taco Pasta Express

4 to 6 servings

prep: 5 minutes   cook: 15 minutes

2   cups uncooked medium pasta shells

1   (16-ounce) package ground pork
        sausage

1   (15-ounce) can chili hot beans
1   (10-ounce) can diced tomatoes and
        green chilies, drained
1   (10-ounce) can enchilada sauce
½   (1¼-ounce) package taco seasoning
        mix
1½ cups (6 ounces) shredded Cheddar
        cheese

1 Cook pasta according to package
directions; drain and keep warm.

2 Meanwhile, cook sausage in a large
nonstick skillet over medium-high
heat, stirring until sausage crumbles and
is no longer pink; drain.

3 Return sausage to skillet. Stir in chili
beans and next 3 ingredients; cook
over medium-high heat 3 minutes or
until slightly thickened, stirring occasionally. Add pasta and cheese, stirring until
cheese melts.

TIME-SAVIN' ⏰ TIP

By organizing your meal preparation just right, you
can simplify the steps. Prepare the meat mixture
while the pasta cooks. And by stirring the hot pasta
and cheese in at the end, you have a hot, cheesy
meal in just minutes without having to bake it for
additional time in the oven.

Speedy Pork Tostadas

4 servings

prep: 10 minutes   cook: 8 minutes

4   (8") flour tortillas
2   tablespoons vegetable oil, divided

½   pound pork tenderloin, cut into
        short, thin strips
2   cloves garlic, minced (see tip)
1   teaspoon ground cumin
1   (16-ounce) can pinto beans, drained
½   cup chunky salsa

2   cups shredded romaine lettuce
½   cup (2 ounces) shredded Cheddar
        cheese
1   tomato, chopped
¼   cup sour cream

1 Preheat the oven to 375°. Arrange tortillas on a baking sheet; using 1 tablespoon oil, coat both sides of tortillas. Bake at 375° for 7 to 8 minutes or until golden.

2 While tortillas bake, heat remaining 1 tablespoon oil in a large nonstick skillet over medium-high heat until hot. Add pork, garlic, and cumin; cook 3 minutes or until pork is browned on all sides, stirring often. Add beans and salsa; simmer 4 minutes or until pork is tender.

3 Place tortillas on 4 individual serving plates; arrange lettuce evenly over tortillas. Top tortillas evenly with pork mixture, cheese, tomato, and sour cream.

TIME-SAVIN' TIP

Use minced garlic from a jar to save chopping time. One teaspoon minced garlic equals 2 regular-sized cloves.

Grilled Ham Steaks

4 servings

prep: 5 minutes   cook: 8 minutes

⅓ cup apple jelly
2   tablespoons chili sauce
1   tablespoon cider vinegar
Dash of ground red pepper

1   (1-pound) lean, boneless ham steak
      (about ½" thick)

1 Combine first 4 ingredients in a small saucepan; cook over medium heat until smooth, stirring often.

2 Cut ham in half lengthwise. Slice each half horizontally into 2 (¼" thick) slices.

3 Spray cold grill rack with nonstick cooking spray; preheat the grill to medium-high heat (350° to 400°). Baste ham with jelly mixture; place ham on grill. Grill, covered, 3 to 4 minutes on each side or until ham is thoroughly heated, basting with remaining jelly mixture.

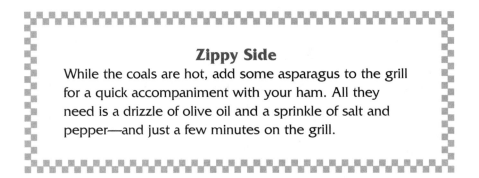

Zippy Side
While the coals are hot, add some asparagus to the grill for a quick accompaniment with your ham. All they need is a drizzle of olive oil and a sprinkle of salt and pepper—and just a few minutes on the grill.

Chicken-Fried Steak

4 servings

prep: 11 minutes   cook: 9 minutes

¼   teaspoon salt
4   (4-ounce) cubed steaks

38   saltine crackers, crushed (about 1
        sleeve)
1   cup self-rising flour
¾   teaspoon ground black pepper

1¾   cups milk, divided
2   large eggs

1   cup peanut oil

1   (2.64-ounce) package country gravy
        mix
1   cup water

1 Sprinkle salt evenly over steaks; set aside.

2 Combine crackers, flour, and pepper in a shallow dish.

3 Whisk together ¾ cup milk and eggs in a separate shallow dish. Dredge steaks in cracker mixture; dip in milk mixture and again in cracker mixture.

4 Pour oil into a 12" skillet (do not use a nonstick skillet); heat oil to 360°. (See tip.) Fry steaks 2 to 3 minutes on each side or until golden. Drain steaks on paper towels.

5 Meanwhile, prepare gravy according to package directions, using remaining 1 cup milk and 1 cup water. Serve over steaks.

"Don't use a nonstick skillet when frying up these golden, delicious steaks—it can't handle the heat and will smoke. Try this indicator to determine if the oil is hot enough to fry. Dust a sprinkling of your flour mixture into the hot oil in the pan. If it sizzles immediately, you're ready to fry!"

Pepper-Beef Stir-Fry

(pictured on page 38)

4 servings

prep: 11 minutes   cook: 10 minutes

1   (5-ounce) package Japanese curly
     noodles (chucka soba) or 5 ounces
     Ramen noodles (without the sea-
     soning packet), uncooked

⅓   cup low-sodium soy sauce
¼   cup beef broth
3   tablespoons dark brown sugar
2   teaspoons cornstarch

1   tablespoon vegetable oil
¾   pound top round steak, thinly sliced

2   teaspoons light sesame oil
2   cloves garlic, minced
1   red bell pepper, cut into thin strips
1   (8-ounce) can sliced water
     chestnuts, drained
3   ounces snow peas, trimmed

1 Cook noodles according to package directions; drain and keep warm.

2 Meanwhile, combine soy sauce and next 3 ingredients in a small bowl; stir well with a whisk. Set aside.

3 Heat 1 tablespoon oil in a large nonstick skillet over medium-high heat until hot; add beef. Stir-fry 4 minutes or until browned. Remove beef from pan; set aside, and keep warm.

4 Coat skillet with 2 teaspoons sesame oil. Add garlic and bell pepper; stir-fry 2 minutes. Add water chestnuts and snow peas; stir-fry 1 minute. Return beef to skillet, and add soy sauce mixture; cook 30 seconds or until slightly thickened. Serve over noodles.

Chinese Takeout from Home

Fresh pineapple complements this flavorful Asian dish. You can buy it already prepared in the produce department of your supermarket. It's great plain, or dress it up by topping with a dollop of sour cream and a sprinkle of brown sugar.

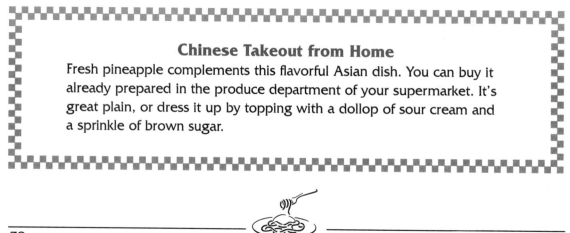

Sirloin Tips with Vegetables

4 servings

prep: 10 minutes   cook: 15 minutes

2	teaspoons olive oil
1	pound sirloin tips
¾	teaspoon salt, divided
¼	teaspoon freshly ground black pepper
1	large Vidalia or other sweet onion, cut into 1½" pieces
1	green bell pepper, cut into 1½" pieces
1	red bell pepper, cut into 1½" pieces
¼	cup plus 2 tablespoons water, divided
2	teaspoons tomato, basil, and garlic seasoning blend or herb-seasoning blend

1 Heat oil in a large nonstick skillet over high heat. Sprinkle sirloin tips with ¼ teaspoon salt and the pepper. Add beef to skillet, and cook 3 to 5 minutes or to desired degree of doneness, stirring often. Remove beef from skillet; set aside, and keep warm.

2 Reduce heat to medium-high. Add onion and bell peppers to skillet; sauté 3 minutes. Add 2 tablespoons water; cook 1 minute.

3 Add beef to onion mixture; sprinkle with seasoning blend and remaining ½ teaspoon salt. Add remaining ¼ cup water to skillet; bring to a boil, scraping browned bits from bottom of skillet. Cook, stirring constantly, 1 minute.

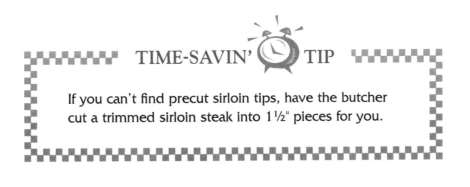

TIME-SAVIN' TIP

If you can't find precut sirloin tips, have the butcher cut a trimmed sirloin steak into 1½" pieces for you.

Hot Beef 'n' Pepper Sandwiches

4 servings

prep: 10 minutes   cook: 7 minutes

1   tablespoon olive oil
½   pound thinly sliced lean roast beef,
           cut into strips
1   large red bell pepper, thinly sliced
1   large green bell pepper, thinly sliced
1   large onion, thinly sliced

4   steak or hoagie rolls, split and
           warmed

1 Heat olive oil in a large nonstick skillet over medium-high heat until hot. Add roast beef, peppers, and onion; sauté until meat is hot and onion is tender.

2 Spoon beef mixture evenly onto bottom halves of rolls, and top with remaining roll halves.

Leftover Savvy

This is a great way to make a meal from leftover roast beef. But if roast beef isn't on your menu this week, pick up ½ pound from your deli.

Sweet 'n' Savory Burgers

8 servings

prep: 15 minutes   chill: 4 hours   cook: 10 minutes

¼   cup soy sauce
2   tablespoons corn syrup
1   tablespoon lemon juice
½   teaspoon ground ginger
¼   teaspoon garlic powder
2   green onions, thinly sliced

2   pounds ground beef

¼   cup chili sauce
¼   cup hot jalapeño jelly
8   hamburger buns

1 Stir together first 6 ingredients; pour into a shallow pan or baking dish.

2 Shape beef into 8 patties; place in a single layer in marinade, turning to coat both sides. Cover and chill 4 hours. Drain, reserving marinade. Bring marinade to a boil in a small saucepan; set aside for basting.

3 Preheat the grill to medium-high heat (350° to 400°). Grill patties 5 minutes on each side or until beef is no longer pink, brushing several times with reserved marinade.

4 Stir together chili sauce and jelly. Serve patties on buns with chili sauce mixture.

TIME-SAVIN' TIP

For great tastin' toppings in no time, toss sweet onion slices and pineapple slices on the grill to cook along with your burgers.

Easy Beefy Casserole

4 to 6 servings

prep: 15 minutes   cook: 30 minutes

1   pound ground beef
¼   teaspoon salt

½   (16-ounce) package frozen mixed
      vegetables
1   (10¾-ounce) can cream of chicken
      soup, undiluted
1   cup (4 ounces) shredded Cheddar
      cheese
½   (32-ounce) package frozen
      seasoned potato tots

1 Preheat the oven to 400°. Cook ground beef and salt in a large skillet over medium heat, stirring until meat crumbles and is no longer pink; drain. Spoon ground beef into a lightly greased 2½-quart shallow baking dish.

2 Layer frozen vegetables, soup, and cheese over ground beef. Top with frozen potatoes.

3 Bake casserole, uncovered, at 400° for 30 minutes or until potatoes are golden.

"You've got all you need in this one-dish wonder— meat, potatoes, and veggies. The kids will be all smiles when you serve this yummy casserole."

Meaty Pizzeria Pie

4 servings

prep: 10 minutes   cook: 30 minutes

1   (15-ounce) package refrigerated pie
    crusts
2   cups spaghetti meat sauce (see tip)
16 pepperoni slices

1   cup (4 ounces) shredded
    mozzarella cheese

1 Preheat the oven to 425°. Unfold pie crusts; stack pie crusts, and press together. Place pie crust on a parchment paper-lined baking sheet. (Do not use wax paper.) Spread spaghetti meat sauce evenly over crust, leaving a 1" border; top with pepperoni slices. Fold crust edges slightly over filling.

2 Bake on lower rack at 425° for 15 minutes. Sprinkle with cheese, and bake 15 more minutes or until bubbly and golden. Cool 5 minutes. Cut into wedges.

Satisfying Leftovers

We recommend using your family's favorite homemade leftover spaghetti meat sauce for this hearty weeknight meal, but your favorite jarred sauce will do just as well. A green salad serves as a simple side for this delicious pie.

Stuffed Peppers

5 servings

prep: 10 minutes   cook: 20 minutes

5   medium-sized green or red bell
       peppers

1   pound lean ground beef
1   medium onion, chopped

1   (15-ounce) can Italian-style tomato
       sauce
1 ¼   teaspoons crushed red pepper
1   teaspoon garlic salt
½   teaspoon black pepper

½   cup shredded Parmesan cheese

1 Cut tops off bell peppers, and reserve tops; remove and discard seeds and membranes. Cook peppers in boiling salted water 4 minutes or until crisp-tender; drain.

2 Coarsely chop reserved pepper tops. Cook chopped pepper, beef, and onion in a large nonstick skillet over medium-high heat until meat crumbles and is no longer pink; drain.

3 Return meat mixture to skillet; stir in tomato sauce and next 3 ingredients; cook over medium-high heat 3 minutes or until mixture thickens.

4 Carefully spoon meat mixture into peppers. Sprinkle with cheese.

TIME-SAVIN' TIPS

Quickly chop bell pepper tops with ease using this little trick: Simply trim the pepper rim away from the stem with 4 strokes in a squarelike pattern; then continue to chop pepper.

Sprinkling the cheese over the hot meat filling as soon as you fill the peppers helps the cheese melt instantly, eliminating an extra step!

Tacos Wrapidos

8 servings

prep: 7 minutes   cook: 12 minutes

1 (5.6-ounce) package Spanish rice
     and pasta blend

1 pound ground chuck
2 teaspoons fajita seasoning

8 (10") flour tortillas
1 avocado, thinly sliced
1½ cups (6 ounces) shredded Cheddar
     cheese
1 cup shredded iceberg lettuce
1 medium tomato, diced

1 Prepare rice according to package directions.

2 Meanwhile, toss ground chuck with fajita seasoning. Cook ground chuck mixture in a large nonstick skillet over medium-high heat, stirring until meat crumbles and is no longer pink; drain.

3 Divide rice evenly over each tortilla. Top evenly with ground chuck, avocado slices, cheese, lettuce, and tomato; roll up tortillas.

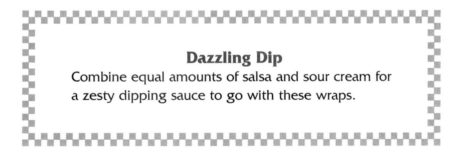

Dazzling Dip
Combine equal amounts of salsa and sour cream for a zesty dipping sauce to go with these wraps.

Easy Skillet Eggplant Lasagna

4 servings

prep: 10 minutes   cook: 18 minutes

1   cup Italian-seasoned
      breadcrumbs
1   (1-pound) eggplant, cut into
      ¼" slices
2   large eggs, beaten

¼   cup vegetable oil, divided

1   (26-ounce) jar marinara sauce
1   cup (4 ounces) shredded mozzarella
      cheese

Mama mia! This super quick Italian favorite is great served alone or on an Italian roll for sandwiches. Either way, you've got a winner!

1 Place breadcrumbs in a shallow dish. Dip eggplant slices in eggs; dredge in breadcrumbs, shaking off excess.

2 Heat 2 tablespoons oil in a large skillet over medium heat until hot. Fry half of eggplant slices in hot oil until golden on each side. Remove from skillet; keep warm. Add remaining oil to skillet; fry remaining eggplant slices until golden on each side. Return reserved eggplant slices to skillet.

3 Pour marinara sauce over eggplant. Bring to a boil; cover, reduce heat, and simmer 5 minutes or until eggplant is tender. Sprinkle with cheese; cover and simmer 1 to 2 more minutes or until cheese melts.

Focaccia Sandwich

(pictured on page 39)

6 servings

prep: 15 minutes   cook: 8 minutes

1   (9") round loaf focaccia

¾   cup roasted pepper dressing,
        divided (see tip)
1   (3-ounce) goat cheese log,
        crumbled, or 4 ounces provolone
        cheese
¼   cup pine nuts or slivered almonds

1   rotisserie chicken
3   cups gourmet salad greens
½   pint grape or cherry tomatoes,
        halved

1 Preheat the oven to 400°. Cut focaccia in half horizontally, using a serrated knife; place cut sides up on a baking sheet.

2 Drizzle ½ cup dressing evenly over cut sides of bread. Sprinkle with goat cheese and nuts. Bake at 400° for 6 to 8 minutes or until lightly browned.

3 Remove meat from chicken, and coarsely chop. Sprinkle chicken over bottom half of bread. Top with salad greens, tomatoes, and remaining ¼ cup dressing; cover with top half of bread. Cut into 6 wedges, and serve immediately.

TIME-SAVIN' TIP

This gourmet sandwich meal is quick and easy. Pick up a rotisserie chicken, prepared dressing, cheese, and some fruit from the supermarket, and dinner is as good as ready! If you can't find the dressing, it's real easy to whip up. Combine ¾ cup of oil-and-vinegar dressing with a 5.2-ounce jar of drained roasted red bell peppers in a food processor, and process until smooth.

The Ultimate Grilled Cheese

5 sandwiches

prep: 5 minutes   cook: 10 minutes

¾ cup mayonnaise

1 (3-ounce) package cream cheese, softened

1 cup (4 ounces) shredded Cheddar cheese

1 cup (4 ounces) shredded mozzarella cheese

½ teaspoon garlic powder

⅛ teaspoon seasoned salt

10 (½") slices sourdough bread

2 tablespoons butter, softened

1 Beat mayonnaise and cream cheese at medium speed of an electric beater until light and fluffy. Stir in Cheddar cheese and next 3 ingredients.

2 Spread each of 5 bread slices evenly with cheese mixture. Top with remaining bread slices.

3 Spread butter on both sides of sandwiches. Cook in batches in skillet over medium heat until lightly browned on both sides. Serve immediately.

"Three kinds of cheese sandwiched between two slices of perfectly golden brown sourdough just beg to be eaten with a bowl of your favorite soup. Check out my favorites starting on page 114."

Speedy Sideshows

66Yes sirree, you can round out your meal in no time with any one—or two—of these speedy side sensations.99

Spiced Apples

4 servings

prep: 10 minutes   cook: 15 minutes

¼ cup butter
4 large Granny Smith apples, peeled,
   cored, and sliced (see tip)
¾ cup sugar
¾ teaspoon ground cinnamon
¼ teaspoon ground nutmeg

1 Melt butter in a large skillet over medium-high heat; add apples and remaining ingredients. Sauté 15 minutes or until apples are tender.

TIME-SAVIN' TIP

Leave the peel on the apples to save time. Granny Smith apples have a firm, juicy flesh that's sweet and tart. They're perfect for sautéing, baking, or eating out-of-hand.

Sugared Asparagus

(pictured on page 2)

3 servings

prep: 5 minutes   cook: 17 minutes

1   pound fresh asparagus

1½   tablespoons butter
1   tablespoon light brown sugar
¼   cup chicken broth

1 Snap off tough ends of asparagus; cut asparagus into 2" pieces.

2 Melt butter and brown sugar in a skillet over medium-high heat, stirring until sugar dissolves. Add asparagus, and sauté in butter mixture 2 minutes. Stir in chicken broth; bring to a boil. Cover, reduce heat, and simmer 4 to 6 minutes or until asparagus is crisp-tender. Remove asparagus to a serving dish; keep warm.

3 Cook sauce, uncovered, until reduced by half. Pour over asparagus, and serve immediately.

"When buying asparagus, always choose firm, bright green stalks with tight tips. Peak season for asparagus is February through June when pencil-thin stalks are plentiful. Later, spears become thicker and aren't as tender when cooked."

Easy Broccoli Casserole

8 servings

prep: 10 minutes   cook: 12 minutes

2 (12-ounce) packages fresh broccoli florets

¼ cup chicken broth

1 (10¾-ounce) can cream of mushroom soup, undiluted

1 (7-ounce) jar roasted red bell peppers, drained and chopped

½ cup (2 ounces) shredded sharp Cheddar cheese

¼ cup mayonnaise

1½ teaspoons lemon juice

1 teaspoon garlic powder

½ teaspoon black pepper

2 tablespoons Italian-seasoned breadcrumbs

1 Combine broccoli and broth in a lightly greased 2-quart baking dish. Cover tightly with heavy-duty plastic wrap, and microwave at HIGH 7 minutes.

2 Combine soup and next 6 ingredients in a medium bowl; stir well. Spoon over broccoli mixture.

3 Sprinkle with breadcrumbs. Cover with heavy-duty plastic wrap, and microwave at HIGH 4 to 5 minutes.

TIME-SAVIN' TIP

Using broccoli florets shortens cook time. These bite-size morsels are sold fresh or frozen. They're so convenient to use for a quick weeknight side.

Carrot Relish

2½ cups

prep: 15 minutes   cook: 18 minutes

1   pound fresh carrots, peeled and
        diced (see tip)

¼   cup chopped green bell pepper
1   (2-ounce) jar diced pimientos,
        drained
¼   cup sugar
¼   cup white vinegar
1   tablespoon all-purpose flour
3   tablespoons honey
¼   teaspoon salt
¼   teaspoon ground red pepper
¼   teaspoon dry mustard
¼   teaspoon celery salt

1 Cook carrots in boiling water to cover in a medium saucepan 8 to 10 minutes or until tender; drain carrots, and return to saucepan.

2 Stir in bell pepper and remaining ingredients; bring to a boil over medium heat, stirring constantly. Reduce heat, and simmer, stirring occasionally, 3 minutes. Serve warm or cold.

TIME-SAVIN' TIP

Pick up a package of fresh carrot sticks from the produce section to speed up prep time. It makes dicing so much easier because no peeling or scraping is necessary!

Parmesan Corn on the Cob

4 servings

prep: 5 minutes   cook: 9 minutes

4	ears fresh corn
¼	cup water
¼	cup butter, softened
¼	cup grated Parmesan cheese
½	teaspoon dried Italian seasoning
½	teaspoon salt

1 Remove and discard husks and silks from corn; place corn in a microwave-safe dish. Add water; cover and microwave at HIGH 8 to 9 minutes or until tender. Drain.

2 Combine butter, Parmesan cheese, and Italian seasoning in a small bowl. Brush butter mixture over corn; sprinkle corn evenly with salt.

"There are a number of ways to prepare fresh corn on the cob—boiled, steamed, grilled—but I like the quickness of the microwave and the fact that the nutrients are retained when foods are cooked in the microwave. Whichever way you prepare it, the Parmesan cheese and Italian seasoning snap your taste buds to attention!"

Lemony Green Beans

3 to 4 servings

prep: 10 minutes   cook: 12 minutes

1	quart water
½	teaspoon salt
1	pound fresh green beans
2	tablespoons butter
1	tablespoon grated lemon rind
1 ½	teaspoons lemon juice
½	teaspoon pepper

1 Bring 1 quart water to a boil in a Dutch oven; add salt and beans. Cook 6 minutes; drain. Plunge into ice water to stop the cooking process; drain.

2 Melt butter in Dutch oven over medium heat; add beans, and sauté 2 minutes. Add lemon rind, and sauté 1 minute. Stir in lemon juice and pepper. Serve immediately.

"If you want to get fancy schmancy, use those French-style green beans. They're oh-so-thin, elegant, and delicate."

Black-Eyed Peas

4 servings

prep: 15 minutes   cook: 10 minutes

2   (15.8-ounce) cans black-eyed peas, drained
6   bacon slices, cooked and crumbled
1   (14-ounce) can chicken broth
1   medium onion, chopped
1   clove garlic, finely chopped
1   bay leaf
¼   teaspoon salt
¼   teaspoon pepper
¼   teaspoon hot sauce

1 Stir together all ingredients in a 2-quart baking dish, mixing well. Cover with heavy-duty plastic wrap, turning back a corner to vent.

2 Microwave at MEDIUM (50% power) 10 minutes; stir well. Let stand, covered, 5 minutes. **Remove and discard bay leaf.**

"With minimal effort, you can have this old-fashioned side ready in 25 minutes—max!"

Smashed Pinto Beans

4 to 6 servings

prep: 15 minutes   cook: 15 minutes

1   teaspoon olive oil
1   medium onion, chopped

½   cup roasted garlic tomato sauce
2   (15-ounce) cans pinto beans, rinsed
       and drained
1   cup beef broth
1   to 2 tablespoons red wine vinegar
1   tablespoon hot sauce
½   teaspoon pepper
¼   teaspoon salt
¼   teaspoon ground cumin

1 Heat olive oil in a Dutch oven over medium-high heat. Add onion, and sauté 5 minutes or until onion is tender.

2 Stir in tomato sauce and remaining ingredients. Bring to a boil; reduce heat, and simmer 8 minutes.

3 Mash bean mixture with a potato masher until thickened, leaving some beans whole.

TIME-SAVIN' TIP

Keep these slightly spicy, fiber-rich beans on hand for quick breakfast burritos or soft veggie tacos.

Grilled Shiitakes

4 servings

prep: 5 minutes   cook: 8 minutes

1	pound large fresh shiitake mushrooms (about 2 dozen)
½	cup butter, melted
4	cloves garlic, minced
¼	cup chopped fresh parsley
½	teaspoon freshly ground pepper
¼	teaspoon salt

1 Remove stems from mushrooms; discard. Combine butter and next 4 ingredients; spread evenly on both sides of mushroom caps.

2 Preheat the grill to medium-high heat (350° to 400°). Grill mushrooms, uncovered, about 8 minutes, turning once. Serve immediately.

TIME-SAVIN' TIP

Add kitchen shears to your must-have list of handy kitchen gadgets. Use them to remove stems from the shiitake mushrooms. Another handy item is a grill rack. It keeps small vegetables and meat cuts from falling into the fire.

Nutty Okra

4 servings

prep: 10 minutes   cook: 4 minutes per batch

1   cup biscuit baking mix
½   cup finely chopped dry-roasted,
       salted peanuts
1   teaspoon salt
½   teaspoon pepper
1   (16-ounce) package frozen cut okra,
       thawed

Peanut oil

1 Stir together biscuit baking mix, chopped peanuts, salt, and pepper in a large bowl. Add okra, tossing to coat; gently press peanut mixture into okra.

2 Pour oil to a depth of 2" into a Dutch oven or cast-iron skillet; heat to 375°. (See tip on page 77.) Fry okra, in batches, 4 minutes or until golden; drain on paper towels.

TIME-SAVIN' TIP

Use a food processor or manual food chopper to chop the peanuts—it does the job fast!

Garlic-Gruyère Mashed Potatoes

4 servings

prep: 7 minutes   cook: 12 minutes

1½ pounds Yukon gold potatoes
       (see tip)

6   tablespoons hot milk
¼   cup sour cream
2   tablespoons butter, softened
½   teaspoon salt
⅛   teaspoon pepper
1   clove garlic, minced

1   cup (4 ounces) shredded Gruyère
       or other Swiss cheese
2   green onions, thinly sliced

1 Peel potatoes; cut into 1" cubes. Cook in boiling water to cover 12 minutes or until tender. Drain.

2 Mash potatoes with a potato masher; stir in milk and next 5 ingredients until blended.

3 Stir in cheese and green onions.

TIME-SAVIN' TIP

Yukon gold potatoes have a naturally yellow color and a rich, buttery-tasting flavor—making excellent mashed potatoes. They can also be baked, sautéed, or fried.

Save time by having all the ingredients measured out so that, while the potatoes are hot, you can add the remaining ingredients, and the cheese will melt easily. Drain the potato water (while hot) into a heat-proof serving bowl. Let sit for a few minutes while you mix everything together. Then pour out, rinse bowl, and spoon in hot mashed potatoes. This trick helps your potatoes stay warm for serving.

Roasted New Potatoes

4 to 6 servings

prep: 10 minutes   cook: 30 minutes

1	large clove garlic, minced
1	teaspoon salt
¼	teaspoon paprika
¼	teaspoon dried rosemary, crushed
⅛	teaspoon pepper
1½	tablespoons olive oil
1½	pounds small red potatoes, cut in half

1 Preheat the oven to 450°. Combine first 6 ingredients in a large bowl. Add potatoes; toss well.

2 Spoon potato mixture onto a lightly greased 10" x 15" rimmed baking sheet. Bake at 450° for 30 minutes or until tender and brown, stirring after 20 minutes.

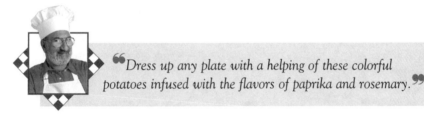

"Dress up any plate with a helping of these colorful potatoes infused with the flavors of paprika and rosemary."

Sweet Potato Casserole

6 servings

prep: 5 minutes   cook: 30 minutes

2   (14½-ounce) cans mashed sweet
      potatoes
½   cup packed dark brown sugar
1   cup evaporated milk
¼   cup butter, melted
1   large egg
3   tablespoons all-purpose flour
½   teaspoon pumpkin pie spice
¼   teaspoon salt

¼   cup chopped pecans

1 Preheat the oven to 350°. Stir together first 8 ingredients; spoon into a lightly greased shallow 2-quart baking dish.

2 Bake at 350° for 30 minutes or until a knife inserted in center comes out clean. Sprinkle with chopped pecans.

"All I have to say is 'Sweet Potato Casserole' and 'family favorite' comes to mind. I'm betting this will become an instant classic with your family, too!"

Baby Spinach with Pine Nuts

4 servings

prep: 5 minutes   cook: 5 minutes

2   (7-ounce) packages baby spinach
2   cloves garlic, minced
1   teaspoon olive oil

¼   teaspoon salt
¼   teaspoon pepper
2   tablespoons pine nuts, toasted
    (see tip below and on page 112)

1 Sauté spinach and garlic in hot oil in a large nonstick skillet over medium-high heat 5 minutes or until spinach wilts.

2 Stir in salt and pepper; sprinkle with pine nuts. Serve immediately.

"Pine nuts are most famous as a key ingredient in pesto; they're also a fine addition to baked goods, desserts, and salads. But they're kinda pricey, so use equal amounts of chopped, toasted pecans or toasted sliced almonds instead, if you like."

Spicy Tomato Macaroni and Cheese

(pictured on facing page)

4 to 6 servings

prep: 7 minutes   cook: 13 minutes

8   ounces uncooked penne pasta

¼   cup butter
½   medium-sized sweet onion,
        chopped
1   (8-ounce) loaf Mexican-style
        pasteurized prepared cheese
        product, cubed
1   (8-ounce) container sour cream

1   (10-ounce) can diced tomatoes and
        green chilies, drained

1 Cook pasta according to package directions; drain well.

2 Meanwhile, melt butter in a large skillet over medium heat; add onion, and sauté 3 minutes or until tender. Add cheese, and cook, stirring constantly, 5 minutes or until cheese melts. Stir in sour cream, blending well.

3 Stir in tomatoes and green chilies and pasta; cook, stirring constantly, 5 minutes or until thoroughly heated.

"To tame the spiciness, switch to regular prepared cheese product and mild diced tomatoes and green chilies. You'll get all the flavor with just a slight kick!"

Zippy Black-Bean Chili and
Broccoli Cornbread Muffins,
pages 120 and 137

Bananas Foster Pancakes,
page 141

Brown Rice with Nuts and Raisins

(pictured on facing page)

4 servings

prep: 15 minutes   cook: 15 minutes

½   cup golden raisins
½   cup dry white wine or ¼ cup
     chicken broth

¼   cup butter
¼   cup chopped onion
2   cups uncooked instant brown rice
1   (14-ounce) can chicken broth
¼   cup water
½   teaspoon salt
¼   teaspoon pepper

¾   cup slivered almonds, toasted
½   cup chopped fresh cilantro or fresh
     mint

1 Combine raisins and wine in a small bowl.

2 Melt butter in a medium skillet over low heat. Add onion; cook, stirring constantly, over medium-high heat until tender. Add rice; cook, stirring constantly, 3 minutes or until lightly browned. Add 1 can broth, the water, salt, and pepper; bring to a boil. Cover, reduce heat, and simmer 10 minutes or until liquid is absorbed.

3 Drain raisins, discarding liquid; stir raisins into rice mixture. Add almonds and cilantro, stirring well.

I cook the rice in chicken broth to give it more flavor and add toasted almonds and cilantro for variety. The raisins are plumped by sitting in the wine or chicken broth, so you don't want to leave that step out or you'll have dry, chewy raisins.

Tex-Mex Rice with Corn

3 servings

prep: 6 minutes   cook: 15 minutes

⅓   cup chopped onion
½   teaspoon minced garlic
1   tablespoon olive oil

1   (5.4-ounce) package Mexican-
      flavored rice orzo blend
1½ cups water
½   cup chunky salsa
½   cup frozen whole kernel corn
½   cup shredded Cheddar cheese

1 Sauté onion and garlic in hot oil in a medium saucepan over medium-high heat 3 minutes.

2 Add rice and next 3 ingredients; bring to a boil. Reduce heat to low; cover and simmer 7 minutes or until rice is tender and most of water is absorbed. Sprinkle with cheese; cover and let stand 3 minutes or until cheese is melted.

"Jazz up a weeknight dinner with this Tex-Mex-inspired side. Serve it alongside quesadillas, and you've got a winner!"

Quick Double-Cheese Grits

8 servings

prep: 5 minutes   cook: 5 minutes

6   cups water
½   teaspoon salt
1½   cups quick-cooking grits

1   cup (4 ounces) shredded extra-
     sharp Cheddar cheese
1   cup (4 ounces) shredded
     Monterey Jack cheese
2   tablespoons butter
½   teaspoon pepper

1 Bring 6 cups water and salt to a boil in a large saucepan. Gradually stir in grits. Cook 4 to 5 minutes until thickened, stirring often. Remove from heat.

2 Add shredded cheeses, butter, and pepper, stirring until blended. Serve immediately.

TIME-SAVIN' TIP

Grits can be made ahead, chilled, and reheated. To reheat, whisk a couple of tablespoons of warm water into grits over medium heat, adding more water as necessary.

Nutty Mint Bulgur

4 servings

prep: 7 minutes   cook: 10 minutes

1½ cups water
¾   teaspoon salt
1   cup uncooked bulgur wheat

3   tablespoons chopped almonds,
      toasted (see tip)
3   tablespoons chopped walnuts,
      toasted (see tip)
2   tablespoons pine nuts, toasted
      (see tip)
2   green onions, sliced
1   tablespoon minced fresh mint

1 Bring 1½ cups water and salt to a boil in a medium saucepan. Stir in bulgur. Cover, reduce heat, and simmer 10 minutes or until tender.

2 Stir in toasted almonds and remaining ingredients. Serve immediately.

TIME-SAVIN' TIP

This Middle Eastern staple has a nutty flavor and a tender but chewy texture. Bulgur is a great way to add nutrients and fiber to your diet. You can find bulgur in the rice aisle of the supermarket.

To speed up prep time, toast nuts ahead and store in an airtight container until you're ready to use them. Simply place them in a skillet over medium-high heat, and cook 2 to 3 minutes, stirring constantly, or until toasted.

Soup and Salad Bar Express

"No long hours of waiting or preparation for these hearty selections of soups and salads. They can be served pronto—the perfect solution to dinner on the double!"

Strawberry-Melon Soup

10 cups

prep: 15 minutes

1	ripe cantaloupe, cubed (about 6¼ cups)
1	pint fresh strawberries, hulled
4	cups orange juice, divided
3	tablespoons lemon juice
1	tablespoon strawberry liqueur (optional)
¼	teaspoon ground ginger

1 Process half of cantaloupe, half of strawberries, and ½ cup orange juice in a food processor or blender until smooth, stopping occasionally to scrape down sides. Pour into a 2½-quart pitcher; set aside. Process remaining cantaloupe and strawberries, and ½ cup orange juice; add to pitcher.

2 Add remaining 3 cups orange juice, the lemon juice, liqueur, if desired, and ginger to pitcher, stirring well. Cover and chill until ready to serve.

TIME-SAVIN' TIP

Your supermarket produce department should have a wide selection of already-cut fruit. And it's also a great place to pick up precut vegetables—they're real time-savers.

Cold Zucchini Soup

8 cups

prep: 13 minutes   cook: 20 minutes   chill: 8 hours

4   medium zucchini, quartered and
        sliced
4   cups chicken broth
4   green onions, chopped
1   teaspoon salt
½   teaspoon pepper
2   (8-ounce) packages cream cheese,
        softened
1   tablespoon chopped fresh dill

1   (8-ounce) container sour cream

1 Combine first 5 ingredients in a saucepan; cook over medium-high heat 20 minutes, stirring occasionally. Add cream cheese and dill.

2 Process mixture, in batches, in a blender until smooth. Stir in sour cream. Cover and chill 8 hours.

66At the first hint of spring, I think, 'cold soup.' This creamy concoction is the perfect opening course for spring and summer get-togethers. And the best part is, you can make it ahead!99

Spinach Egg Drop Soup

6 cups

prep: 5 minutes   cook: 5 minutes

6   cups chicken broth
1   large egg, lightly beaten

1   tablespoon soy sauce
½   teaspoon sugar
2   green onions, chopped
2   cups torn fresh spinach

1 Bring broth to a boil; reduce heat to a simmer. Slowly add egg, stirring constantly, until egg forms lacy strands. Immediately remove from heat. Let stand 1 minute.

2 Stir in soy sauce, sugar, and green onions. Divide spinach among 6 bowls; ladle soup over spinach. Serve immediately.

"For eye appeal and extra texture, flavor, and color, I like to add sliced fresh shiitake or button mushrooms and thinly sliced red bell pepper. Sprinkle them into the empty bowls along with the spinach, ladle soup into bowls— and enjoy!"

Roasted Garlic-Potato Soup

4 cups

prep: 8 minutes   cook: 5 minutes

2   cups milk
1½   cups water
½   (7.6-ounce) package roasted garlic
        instant mashed potatoes

1   cup (4 ounces) shredded sharp
        Cheddar cheese, divided
¼   teaspoon freshly ground pepper

1 Combine milk and water in a large saucepan; bring to a boil. Remove from heat; add potatoes, and stir with a wire whisk until well blended.

2 Add ¾ cup cheese, stirring until cheese melts. Spoon into 4 bowls; sprinkle with remaining ¼ cup cheese and the pepper.

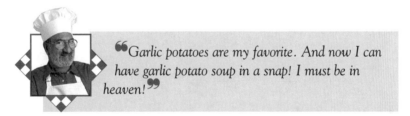

"Garlic potatoes are my favorite. And now I can have garlic potato soup in a snap! I must be in heaven!"

Lobster and Chive Bisque

5 cups

prep: 7 minutes   cook: 20 minutes

3   tablespoons butter
1   tablespoon minced onion
3   tablespoons all-purpose flour

3   cups milk
1   cup heavy whipping cream
½   cup dry sherry or chicken broth
1   teaspoon salt
⅛   teaspoon paprika
1   cup cooked lobster meat (about
       1 pound)
2   tablespoons chopped fresh chives or
       2 teaspoons dried chives

1 Melt butter in a Dutch oven over medium heat. Sauté minced onion 1 minute or until tender. Add flour, stirring until blended. Cook 1 minute, stirring constantly.

2 Gradually add milk and next 4 ingredients. Bring just to a simmer; cook, uncovered, 15 to 18 minutes or until slightly thickened (do not boil). Stir in lobster and chives.

"Serve this fancy bisque with breadsticks and a simple green salad for an oh-so-quick meal! And if lobster is not in your budget, try substituting an equal amount of surimi. Available in the seafood sections of most supermarkets, surimi is made from mild, white-fleshed fish and is colored and flavored to resemble various types of shellfish."

Mexican Chicken-Corn Chowder

9 cups

prep: 5 minutes   cook: 15 minutes

3   tablespoons butter
½   cup chopped onion
1   clove garlic, minced

4   cups chopped cooked chicken
1   cup chicken broth
½   teaspoon ground cumin

2   cups half-and-half
1   (4.5-ounce) can chopped green
        chilies
2   cups (8 ounces) shredded Monterey
        Jack cheese with peppers

1 Melt butter in a Dutch oven over medium heat. Sauté onion and garlic 3 minutes or until tender.

2 Add chicken, broth, and cumin. Bring to a boil; cover, reduce heat, and simmer 3 minutes.

3 Add half-and-half, chilies, and cheese. Cook over low heat until thoroughly heated. Serve immediately.

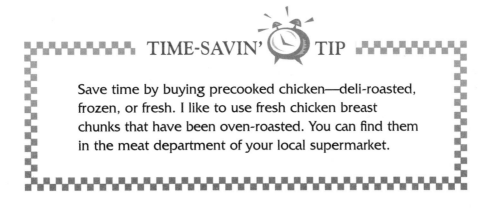

TIME-SAVIN' TIP

Save time by buying precooked chicken—deli-roasted, frozen, or fresh. I like to use fresh chicken breast chunks that have been oven-roasted. You can find them in the meat department of your local supermarket.

Zippy Black-Bean Chili

(pictured on page 106)

4 cups

prep: 3 minutes   cook: 16 minutes

¾   pound ground beef
1   tablespoon chili powder

1   (19-ounce) can black beans, rinsed
        and drained
1   (14½-ounce) can crushed tomatoes,
        undrained
1   (8-ounce) jar hot salsa
Shredded Cheddar cheese

1 Cook ground beef in a large skillet over medium-high heat, stirring until it crumbles and is no longer pink; drain well. Add chili powder; cook 3 minutes, stirring constantly.

2 Add black beans, tomatoes, and salsa; bring to a boil. Cover, reduce heat, and simmer 5 minutes, stirring constantly. Sprinkle each serving with cheese.

"Here's one of my standbys—a chili that's quick to fix with a flavor that'll have everybody coming back for more."

Brunswick Stew

8 to 10 servings

prep: 5 minutes   cook: 30 minutes

3   cups chicken broth
2   cups chopped cooked chicken
1   (24-ounce) container barbecued
        shredded pork
1   (16-ounce) package frozen
        vegetable gumbo mixture
1   (10-ounce) package frozen corn
½   (10-ounce) package frozen petite
        lima beans
½   cup ketchup

1 Bring all ingredients to a boil in a Dutch oven over medium-high heat, stirring often. Cover, reduce heat to low, and simmer, stirring occasionally, 25 minutes or until thoroughly heated.

TIME-SAVIN' TIP

This cold-weather stew is ready in a snap with the help of convenience products. In certain regions of the country, barbecue is available in the meat department of local supermarkets. If your grocer doesn't have it, drop by a favorite barbecue restaurant and get some shredded pork to go.

Iceberg Wedges with Double Cheese Dressing

4 servings

prep: 7 minutes

Prepared blue cheese dressing
1   medium head iceberg lettuce, cut
        into 4 wedges
6   to 8 bacon slices, cooked and
        crumbled
½   cup shredded Parmesan cheese
¼   cup chopped fresh chives or
        1 tablespoon dried chives

1 Pour dressing over lettuce wedges on individual serving plates. Combine bacon, cheese, and chives; sprinkle over dressing.

TIME-SAVIN' TIP

Save cooking and cleanup time by cooking the bacon in the microwave. Place bacon slices for this recipe on a plate, and cover with paper towels. Microwave on HIGH for 5 to 7 minutes or until crisp. Or better yet, purchase pre-cooked bacon at the supermarket. Also, shave off prep time by using your kitchen shears to snip the fresh chives.

Italian BLT Bread Salad

(pictured on page 3)

6 to 8 servings

prep: 10 minutes   cook: 5 minutes   chill: 1 hour

1	(8-ounce) Italian or French bread loaf, cut into 1" chunks
½	pound fresh mozzarella, cut into ½" pieces
1	cup olive oil-and-balsamic vinegar dressing
½	cup kalamata olives, pitted and halved
1	pint grape tomatoes, halved
2	green onions, sliced
2	tablespoons chopped fresh basil
¼	teaspoon pepper
3	cups chopped romaine lettuce
10	bacon slices, cooked and crumbled

1 Preheat the oven to 400°. Place bread chunks on a baking sheet, and bake at 400° for 5 minutes or until lightly toasted.

2 Combine mozzarella and dressing in a shallow dish or resealable plastic bag; cover or seal, and chill 1 hour.

3 Toss together bread, olives, next 4 ingredients, and mozzarella mixture. Let stand 20 minutes. Serve over lettuce, and sprinkle with crumbled bacon.

TIME-SAVIN' TIP

The oven is a great tool for cooking batches of bacon ahead. Place bacon slices on the rack of a roasting pan, and bake at 400° for 20 to 25 minutes or until crisp. While bacon cooks, you're free to prepare other ingredients. Or, if you're in a super hurry, use your microwave. See the opposite page for tips. Ten slices will take about 7 to 9 minutes in the microwave.

Roasted Onion Salad

8 servings

prep: 15 minutes   cook: 15 minutes

5   medium onions, peeled and cut into
        ½" thick slices
¼   cup olive oil

8   cups gourmet mixed salad greens
½   cup chopped walnuts, toasted
1   (4-ounce) package crumbled blue
        cheese
Prepared garlic vinaigrette

1 Preheat the oven to 450°. Arrange onion slices in a lightly greased roasting pan. Drizzle evenly with olive oil.

2 Bake at 450° for 12 to 15 minutes or until onion slices are lightly roasted. Cool 5 minutes.

3 Combine salad greens, walnuts, and blue cheese; toss gently. Top with onions, and drizzle with garlic vinaigrette.

“When onions are cooked long enough to brown, they caramelize as a result of the natural sugar that's in 'em. It's a magical process that adds rich flavor to this salad.”

"Hot" Spinach Salad

3 to 4 servings

prep: 5 minutes   cook: 6 minutes

¼   cup olive oil
1   (6-ounce) package sliced
     Portobello mushrooms, cut in half
½   medium onion, thinly sliced

¾   cup pitted kalamata olives
6   cherry tomatoes, halved
¼   cup balsamic vinegar
1   (7-ounce) package fresh baby
     spinach

¼   cup crumbled goat cheese or feta
     cheese
¼   teaspoon salt
⅛   teaspoon pepper

1 Heat oil in a large skillet over medium-high heat. Sauté mushrooms and onion 3 minutes or until tender.

2 Reduce heat to low; add olives, tomatoes, and vinegar; cook 3 minutes, stirring occasionally. Toss spinach with mushroom mixture in a large bowl.

3 Place salad on a serving platter; top with goat cheese, and sprinkle with salt and pepper. Serve immediately.

The warm mushroom mixture helps melt the goat cheese to make each bite of this salad extra creamy.

Loaded Veggie Salad

8 to 10 servings

prep: 12 minutes

2   (10-ounce) packages Italian mixed
    salad greens
2   large avocados, chopped
1   large cucumber, sliced
1   pint grape tomatoes
1½ cups shredded carrots
¾   cup sweetened dried cranberries
½   cup sliced almonds, toasted
1   (6-ounce) package crumbled feta
    with tomato and basil

1   cup prepared balsamic vinaigrette

1 Combine first 8 ingredients in a large salad bowl; toss well.

2 Pour vinaigrette over salad mixture, and toss gently. Serve immediately.

"A fun salad with loads of unexpected ingredients. Wow! Fruit, nuts, cheese, and veggies—it's got it all!"

Pizza Pasta Salad

4 to 6 servings

prep: 10 minutes   cook: 9 minutes

8	ounces uncooked rotini pasta
1	(14-ounce) can quartered artichoke hearts, drained
4	ounces sliced pepperoni
6	ounces cubed mozzarella cheese
2	cups grape tomatoes, halved
¼	cup sliced ripe olives
1	(12-ounce) jar roasted red bell peppers, drained
⅓	cup Italian salad dressing
½	cup sliced fresh basil
¼	teaspoon freshly ground black pepper

1 Cook pasta according to package directions; drain and rinse under cold water immediately. Place drained pasta in a large serving bowl.

2 Combine artichoke hearts and next 4 ingredients; set aside.

3 Place roasted peppers in a blender, and process until almost smooth. Stir in salad dressing, basil, and black pepper.

4 Add pepper mixture to pasta; then add artichoke mixture to pasta, and toss well.

TIME-SAVIN' TIP

You can make this salad a day ahead. Just cover and store in the refrigerator until serving time.

Mediterranean Couscous Salad

4 servings

prep: 10 minutes   stand: 5 minutes

1   (14-ounce) can vegetable broth
1   cup uncooked couscous

1   (15-ounce) can chickpeas, drained
4   green onions, sliced
½   cup sweetened dried cranberries,
        raisins, or chopped dried apricots
¼   cup chopped fresh parsley

1   tablespoon grated orange rind
¼   cup orange juice
1   tablespoon vegetable oil
¼   cup crumbled feta cheese

1 Bring broth to a boil in a medium saucepan over medium-high heat. Stir in couscous, and remove from heat. Cover and let stand 5 minutes.

2 Transfer couscous to a bowl, and fluff with a fork. Add chickpeas and next 3 ingredients; toss gently.

3 Whisk together orange rind, orange juice, and oil in a small bowl. Add dressing to salad, and toss well. Sprinkle with feta cheese just before serving. Serve immediately.

TIME-SAVIN' TIP

Couscous is one ingredient that you can prepare in a flash! Just bring liquid to a boil, stir in couscous, and cover for 5 minutes. Add some beans or dried fruit, and you've got a salad in minutes!

Lentil-and-Orzo Salad

4 servings

prep: 15 minutes   chill: 2 hours

¼ cup prepared vinaigrette dressing
2 tablespoons lemon juice
½ teaspoon ground cumin
½ teaspoon salt
½ teaspoon ground black pepper
¼ teaspoon crushed red pepper

2 cups cooked lentils
1 cup cooked orzo
½ red bell pepper, diced
½ small red onion, diced
1½ tablespoons chopped fresh cilantro

1 Whisk together first 6 ingredients in a large bowl.

2 Add lentils and remaining ingredients, tossing gently to coat. Cover and chill 2 hours.

"I call this my international salad. Take a look at what's in it—lentils, orzo (rice-shaped pasta), cumin, and cilantro. I think we covered the globe with this one!"

Margarita Coleslaw

8 to 10 servings

prep: 15 minutes

1 (10-ounce) can frozen margarita
    mix, thawed and undiluted
¼ cup white vinegar
¼ cup vegetable oil
2 tablespoons honey
1 teaspoon celery seeds

9 cups shredded green cabbage
3 cups shredded red cabbage
2 large Granny Smith apples, peeled
    and chopped
1 cup sweetened dried cranberries

1 Whisk together first 5 ingredients in a medium bowl. Cover dressing, and chill until ready to use.

2 Combine green cabbage and next 3 ingredients. Add desired amount of dressing to coleslaw, and toss gently to coat. Serve immediately.

TIME-SAVIN' TIP

Look for shredded cabbage in the produce section of your supermarket. It's usually available in varying widths, from wispy angel hair to matchstick size.

Honey-Pecan Dressing

2½ cups

prep: 5 minutes

½   cup honey
¼   cup red wine vinegar
3   tablespoons sugar
1   tablespoon chopped sweet onion
½   teaspoon dry mustard
¼   teaspoon salt

1   cup vegetable oil
1   cup chopped pecans, toasted

1 Pulse first 6 ingredients in a blender 2 to 3 times until blended.

2 With blender running, pour oil through food chute in a slow, steady stream; process until smooth. Stir in pecans. Use immediately, or store in the refrigerator up to a week.

TIME-SAVIN' TIP

Arrange cut fresh fruit or canned or frozen (thawed) fruit over lettuce leaves, and drizzle with this sweet and tangy dressing. Or serve the dressing over prepackaged salad greens.

Roasted Red Bell Pepper Dressing

about 2 cups

prep: 5 minutes

1   (7-ounce) jar roasted red bell
    peppers, drained
2   cloves garlic, chopped
1   cup plain yogurt
1   teaspoon salt

1 Pulse all ingredients in a blender 5 or 6 times or until smooth.

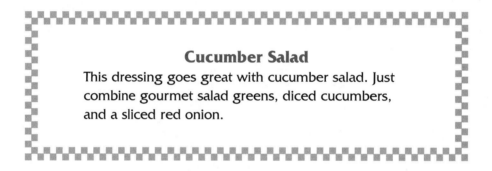

Cucumber Salad

This dressing goes great with cucumber salad. Just combine gourmet salad greens, diced cucumbers, and a sliced red onion.

Time-Savin' Breads

"Mere minutes is all it takes to fill your home with the aroma and goodness of these freshly baked breads."

Rosemary Biscuits

8 biscuits

prep: 8 minutes   cook: 14 minutes

2   cups self-rising flour
1   tablespoon chopped fresh rosemary
    (see tip)
⅓   cup butter
¾   cup buttermilk

¼   cup butter, divided

1 Preheat the oven to 450°. Combine flour and rosemary. Cut ⅓ cup butter into flour mixture with a pastry blender until crumbly; add buttermilk, stirring just until dry ingredients are moistened.

2 Turn dough out onto a lightly floured surface; knead 3 or 4 times.

3 Place 2 tablespoons butter in a 10" cast-iron skillet. Place skillet in 450° oven for 5 minutes.

4 Meanwhile, pat or roll dough to ½" thickness; cut with a 2½" round cutter. Remove skillet from oven, and place dough rounds in skillet.

5 Bake at 450° for 14 minutes or just until lightly browned. Brush with 2 tablespoons melted butter.

Biscuit Basics

• Don't overwork the dough. The key to flaky biscuits is to gently knead dough 3 or 4 times to incorporate air, which creates flakiness.

• If you don't have a cast-iron skillet, these biscuits bake just as nicely on an un-greased baking sheet. Bake at 450° for 14 minutes.

• For plain buttermilk biscuits, simply omit the rosemary.

Sweet Potato Biscuits

14 biscuits

prep: 15 minutes   cook: 13 minutes

4   cups all-purpose flour
2   tablespoons baking powder
2   teaspoons salt
1   cup cold butter

1   (14½-ounce) can cooked mashed
      sweet potato
1   cup buttermilk

1 Preheat the oven to 425°. Combine flour, baking powder, and salt; cut butter into flour mixture with a pastry blender until crumbly.

2 Combine 1 cup sweet potato and buttermilk; add to flour mixture, stirring just until dry ingredients are moistened. (Reserve remaining sweet potato for another use.)

3 Turn dough out onto a lightly floured surface; knead 3 or 4 times. Pat or roll dough to ¾" thickness; cut dough with a 2¾" round cutter, and place on a lightly greased baking sheet.

4 Bake at 425° for 13 minutes or until edges are golden.

Serving Tip

These buttery biscuits are great for breakfast or dinner, and we especially like them as holiday cocktail biscuits—just tuck a few slivers of baked ham and a spoonful of cranberry sauce into each one before baking. If you want to make these biscuits slightly smaller, use a smaller cutter and remember to bake a minute or two less.

Chocolate Buttermilk Biscuits

about 1 dozen

prep: 9 minutes   cook: 15 minutes

3   tablespoons sugar, divided
⅛   teaspoon ground cinnamon

2   cups self-rising flour
⅓   cup butter
¾   cup buttermilk
½   cup semisweet chocolate chips

¼   cup butter, melted

1 Preheat the oven to 425°. Combine 2 tablespoons sugar and the cinnamon; set aside.

2 Combine flour and remaining 1 tablespoon sugar in a large bowl; cut butter into flour mixture with a pastry blender until mixture is crumbly. Add buttermilk and chocolate chips, stirring just until dry ingredients are moistened.

3 Turn dough out onto a lightly floured surface; knead 3 or 4 times. Pat or roll dough to ½" thickness; cut with a 2¼" round cutter. Place biscuits on a baking sheet; sprinkle with sugar mixture.

4 Bake at 425° for 15 minutes or until golden. Brush biscuits with ¼ cup melted butter.

Boy, are these biscuits good—mouthwatering morsels with a hit of chocolate! Bake 'em up for a weekend eye-opener!

Broccoli Cornbread Muffins

(pictured on page 106)

3 dozen

prep: 10 minutes   cook: 12 minutes

1	(8½-ounce) package corn muffin mix
1	(10-ounce) package frozen chopped broccoli, thawed
1	cup (4 ounces) shredded Cheddar cheese
1	small onion, chopped
2	large eggs
½	cup butter, melted

1 Preheat the oven to 375°. Combine first 4 ingredients in a large bowl; make a well in center of mixture.

2 Stir together eggs and butter, blending well; pour into well of broccoli mixture, stirring just until dry ingredients are moistened. Spoon into lightly greased miniature (1¾") muffin pans, filling three-fourths full.

3 Bake at 375° for 12 minutes or until golden. Let stand 2 to 3 minutes before removing from pans.

"Broccoli has never been tastier! It's easy to get in your 'Five a Day' with recipes like my Broccoli Cornbread Muffins. One taste of these savory bites will have 'em coming back for more."

Cheddar-Nut Muffins

1 dozen

prep: 10 minutes   cook: 15 minutes

3¾ cups biscuit baking mix
1½ cups (6 ounces) shredded Cheddar
      cheese

1   large egg
1   (12-ounce) can evaporated milk
½   cup chopped pecans, toasted
      (see tip)

1 Preheat the oven to 375°. Combine biscuit baking mix and cheese in a large bowl; make a well in center of mixture.

2 Stir together egg and milk; pour into well of cheese mixture, stirring just until moistened. Stir in toasted pecans. Spoon mixture into lightly greased muffin pans, filling two-thirds full.

3 Bake at 375° for 12 to 15 minutes. Let stand 2 or 3 minutes before removing from pans.

Nuts about Toasting
Toasting brings out the full flavor of nuts. To toast pecans, place them in a dry skillet over medium heat for 2 to 3 minutes, stirring often.

Sesame-Cheese Muffins

8 muffins

prep: 10 minutes   cook: 23 minutes

1   tablespoon butter
1   small sweet onion, finely chopped

1½ cups biscuit baking mix
1   cup (4 ounces) shredded sharp
       Cheddar cheese, divided

1   large egg
½   cup milk
1   teaspoon sesame seeds, toasted
2   tablespoons butter, melted

1 Preheat the oven to 400°. Melt 1 tablespoon butter in a small skillet over medium-high heat. Add onion, and sauté 2 minutes or until tender; set aside.

2 Combine biscuit baking mix and ½ cup cheese in a large bowl; make a well in center of mixture.

3 Stir together onion, egg, and milk, blending well; pour into well of cheese mixture, stirring just until dry ingredients are moistened. Spoon into lightly greased muffin pans, filling two-thirds full. Sprinkle evenly with remaining cheese and the sesame seeds; drizzle with melted butter.

4 Bake at 400° for 15 to 20 minutes or until golden.

Mini Muffins

Substitute miniature (1¾") muffin pans for regular pans, if desired. Just bake at 400° for 12 to 14 minutes or until golden. Makes 1½ dozen mini muffins.

Chocolate Chip Mini Muffins

3 dozen

prep: 10 minutes   cook: 20 minutes

2   cups self-rising flour
1   (8-ounce) container sour cream
1   cup butter, melted
½   cup semisweet chocolate chips

¼   cup sugar
¼   teaspoon ground cinnamon

1 Preheat the oven to 400°. Combine first 4 ingredients in a large bowl. Spoon batter into lightly greased miniature (1¾") muffin pans, filling full.

2 Combine sugar and cinnamon; sprinkle evenly over muffins.

3 Bake at 400° for 20 minutes or until golden; remove muffins from pans, and cool on wire racks.

"These muffins have just the right amount of chocolate in them so they're not too sweet but ooh so good!"

Bananas Foster Pancakes

(pictured on page 107)

9 (4") pancakes

prep: 4 minutes   cook: 12 minutes

1   (5.5-ounce) package biscuit baking
     mix
1   teaspoon ground cinnamon
1   large ripe banana, mashed

1   cup pure maple syrup
¼   cup dark rum or ½ teaspoon rum
     extract

½   cup chopped pecans, toasted
1   large banana, sliced

1 Prepare biscuit baking mix according to package directions; stir in cinnamon and mashed banana.

2 Pour about ¼ cup batter for each pancake onto a hot, lightly greased griddle. Cook pancakes until tops are covered with bubbles and edges look cooked; turn and cook other side.

3 Meanwhile, heat maple syrup in a small saucepan over medium heat until warmed. Remove from heat; add rum, and stir well.

4 Serve pancakes warm with maple syrup mixture; sprinkle evenly with pecans and banana slices.

“These pancakes are great for breakfast or brunch, but you're gonna like them as dessert, too. All you need for a finishing touch is a topping of ice cream or whipped topping.”

Blueberry-Cream Cheese Pancakes

21 (4") pancakes

prep: 10 minutes   cook: 20 minutes

1   (3-ounce) package cream cheese,
       softened
2   large eggs, lightly beaten

2   cups self-rising flour
2   tablespoons sugar

1¼ to 1½ cups milk
2   tablespoons butter, melted
1½ teaspoons vanilla extract
1½ cups blueberries

1 Beat cream cheese at medium speed of an electric beater until creamy; add eggs, 1 at a time, beating after each addition.

2 Stir together flour and sugar in a large bowl; make a well in center of mixture.

3 Combine cream cheese mixture, milk, butter, and vanilla in a small bowl, stirring well; pour into well of flour mixture, stirring just until dry ingredients are moistened. Stir in blueberries.

4 Pour about ¼ cup batter for each pancake onto a hot, lightly greased griddle. Cook pancakes until tops are covered with bubbles and edges look cooked; turn and cook other side. Serve with warm maple syrup or sifted powdered sugar.

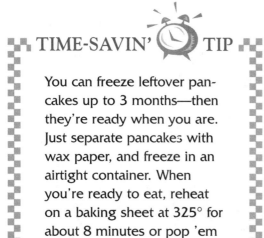

TIME-SAVIN' TIP

You can freeze leftover pancakes up to 3 months—then they're ready when you are. Just separate pancakes with wax paper, and freeze in an airtight container. When you're ready to eat, reheat on a baking sheet at 325° for about 8 minutes or pop 'em in the microwave.

Easy Caramel Rolls

2 dozen

prep: 4 minutes   cook: 20 minutes

3   (8-ounce) cans refrigerated crescent
      rolls

1   cup packed light brown sugar
¾   cup butter
½   cup light corn syrup
1   teaspoon vanilla extract
1   cup chopped pecans, toasted

1 Preheat the oven to 400°. Open crescent roll dough; do not unroll. Slice each roll into 8 (¾"-thick) pieces. Place rolls ¼" apart in a lightly greased 9" x 13" pan. Bake at 400° for 20 minutes or until golden brown and firm.

2 Meanwhile, combine sugar, butter, and corn syrup in a medium saucepan. Cook over medium heat, stirring constantly, until melted and smooth. Remove from heat, and stir in vanilla. Pour sauce over warm rolls; sprinkle with pecans. Serve warm.

"Talk about ooey and gooey! Yum-my! Thank goodness these make 2 dozen—if not, I wouldn't have enough to share."

Mini Cream Cheese Rolls

4 dozen

prep: 14 minutes   cook: 15 minutes

2   (8-ounce) cans refrigerated crescent
      rolls

2   (3-ounce) packages cream cheese,
      softened
2   tablespoons granulated sugar
1   teaspoon lemon juice

1   cup powdered sugar
2   tablespoons milk
1   teaspoon vanilla extract

1 Preheat the oven to 375°. Unroll crescent rolls, and separate each dough portion along center perforation to form 8 rectangles; press diagonal perforations to seal.

2 Stir together cream cheese, granulated sugar, and lemon juice; spread cream cheese mixture evenly over each rectangle. Roll up, jellyroll fashion, starting at long end. Gently cut each log into 6 slices. Place rolls, cut side up, in an ungreased 9" x 13" pan. Bake at 375° for 15 minutes or until lightly browned.

3 Meanwhile, combine powdered sugar and milk in a small bowl; stir in vanilla. Drizzle over warm rolls.

Glazes Galore

Chocolate Glaze: Microwave 1 cup semisweet chocolate chips in a microwave-safe glass bowl at HIGH 1½ minutes or until melted, stirring twice. Drizzle chocolate over warm rolls.

Orange Glaze: Combine 1 cup powdered sugar, 1 teaspoon grated orange rind, 2 tablespoons orange juice, and 1 teaspoon vanilla extract. Drizzle over warm rolls.

Creole Hush Puppies

7 dozen

prep: 15 minutes   cook: 4 minutes per batch

2   large eggs
1¼   cups buttermilk
1   (14⅔-ounce) can cream-style
         corn
1   (10-ounce) can diced tomatoes
         and green chilies, undrained
1   tablespoon Creole seasoning
5   cups self-rising yellow cornmeal
3   medium onions, finely chopped
½   cup finely chopped green bell
         pepper
2   jalapeño peppers, finely chopped
         (see tip)

Vegetable oil

1 Stir together first 5 ingredients. Add cornmeal, and stir just until moistened. Add onions and peppers; stir well.

2 Pour oil to a depth of 2" into a Dutch oven; heat to 360°. (See tip on page 77.) Drop batter by level tablespoonfuls into hot oil; fry hush puppies, a few at a time, 3 to 4 minutes or until golden, turning once.

Here's the Scoop

Use a small ice cream scoop (measures 4 teaspoons) to drop the batter into hot oil for frying. You can also use a measuring tablespoon or a dinner tablespoon, though they might not be quite as round.

These hush puppies freeze well up to 3 months. When you're ready to eat, thaw them in small batches in the microwave at HIGH 1 minute. Then place on a rimmed baking sheet, and bake at 450° for 4 minutes or until crispy.

It's best to use rubber gloves when seeding and chopping jalapeños. The seeds and veins in them are hot and can burn your hands.

Parmesan Crisps

2 dozen

prep: 15 minutes   cook: 8 minutes

1 ½ cups (6 ounces) finely shredded
      Parmesan cheese

1 Preheat the oven to 350°. Sprinkle about 1 tablespoon cheese, forming a 2" round, on an aluminum-foil lined baking sheet coated with nonstick cooking spray. Repeat with remaining cheese, leaving 1" between rounds.

2 Bake at 350° for 8 minutes or until lightly browned. Using a spatula, quickly remove cheese crisps from baking sheet. Cool on a wire rack. Store in an airtight container.

"To add a flavorful crunch to your favorite salad or soup, add these cheesy crisps either whole or crushed. They also make tasty snacks just by themselves. Fresh Parmesan cheese works best for this recipe if time allows."

Crunch Sticks

20 breadsticks

prep: 10 minutes   cook: 10 minutes

1   (12-ounce) can buttermilk biscuits

1½ cups crisp rice cereal, coarsely
        crushed
2   tablespoons caraway seeds
2   tablespoons celery seeds
2   tablespoons dillseeds
1   teaspoon salt
3   tablespoons milk

1 Preheat the oven to 450°. Cut each biscuit in half. Roll each half into a pencil-thin stick.

2 Combine cereal and seasonings in a shallow pan. Brush sticks with milk. Roll sticks in cereal mixture. Place 2" apart on lightly greased baking sheets. Bake at 450° for 8 to 10 minutes or until lightly browned.

"These breadsticks are a snap to make and ooh-so-much better than the store-bought variety. They're great served with any of the soups and salads that begin on page 114 . . . or for just plain snackin'!"

Cinnamon Breadsticks

1 dozen

prep: 14 minutes   cook: 17 minutes

2   (11-ounce) cans refrigerated soft
      breadsticks

1   cup granulated sugar
1   tablespoon ground cinnamon
¼   cup butter, melted

1   cup powdered sugar
2   tablespoons milk
¼   teaspoon vanilla extract

1 Preheat the oven to 350°. Gently twist 2 breadsticks together, pinching ends to seal.

2 Combine granulated sugar and cinnamon on a plate. Brush breadsticks with melted butter, and sprinkle generously with sugar mixture.

3 Place breadsticks on a baking sheet. Bake at 350° for 17 minutes or until lightly browned. Cool on pan 5 minutes; remove to wire racks.

4 Combine powdered sugar and milk in a small bowl; stir in vanilla. Drizzle glaze over warm breadsticks.

Coffee Talk
Bring out these cinnamon delights the next time you have your friends over for coffee. It's a great way to start your day off right.

Blue Cheese Bread

8 servings

prep: 5 minutes   cook: 7 minutes

1   (12-ounce) crusty French bread loaf

½   cup butter, softened
1   (4-ounce) package crumbled blue
         cheese

1 Preheat the oven to 375°. Cut bread loaf at ¾" intervals, cutting to, but not through, bottom of loaf.

2 Stir together butter and cheese; spread evenly on both sides of each bread slice. Wrap loaf in aluminum foil, and place on a baking sheet.

3 Bake at 375° for 7 minutes or until toasted.

❝The bold flavor of blue cheese is a tasty alternative to regular garlic bread. Try this cheesy variation with your next meal and see why it's one of my favorites!❞

Greek Bread

6 servings

prep: 10 minutes   cook: 30 minutes

1½ cups (6 ounces) shredded
      mozzarella cheese
¼   cup butter, softened
2   tablespoons mayonnaise
6   green onions, chopped
1   (2¼-ounce) can sliced ripe olives,
      drained
¼   teaspoon garlic salt
1   (1-pound) loaf Italian bread

1 Preheat the oven to 350°. Stir together er first 6 ingredients until well blended. Cut bread in half lengthwise. Spread butter mixture over each cut side of bread.

2 Wrap bread in aluminum foil, and bake at 350° for 20 minutes. Open foil, and bake bread 10 more minutes or until lightly browned.

❝A hefty slice of this gooey bread that's loaded with olives, onions, and garlic is the perfect go-along with a dinner salad or soup. Make a match with any of the ones starting on page 114.❞

Easy Italian Bread

12 servings

prep: 10 minutes   cook: 20 minutes

1   (32-ounce) package frozen bread
        dough loaves, thawed

2   tablespoons olive oil
2   teaspoons dried Italian seasoning
½   teaspoon garlic powder
¼   cup shredded Parmesan cheese

1 Preheat the oven to 375°. Divide loaves into 3 equal portions. Roll each portion into a 6½" circle, and place on a lightly greased baking sheet.

2 Brush with olive oil, and sprinkle with Italian seasoning, garlic powder, and Parmesan cheese.

3 Bake at 375° for 10 minutes. Prick several times with a fork. Bake 10 more minutes or until golden. Cool slightly on baking sheet. Cut each round into 4 wedges.

"With just 4 ingredients, you can take plain bread from ordinary to spectacular. Now that's so-o-o easy and so-o-o good!"

Southwestern Knots

1 dozen

prep: 5 minutes   cook: 15 minutes

2½ tablespoons butter, melted
¼   teaspoon ground cumin
¼   teaspoon chili powder

1   (11-ounce) can refrigerated
    breadsticks

1 Preheat the oven to 350°. Stir together melted butter, cumin, and chili powder until blended.

2 Unroll breadsticks, and separate each dough portion. Loosely tie each portion into a knot, and place 1" apart on an ungreased baking sheet. Brush evenly with butter mixture.

3 Bake at 350° for 15 minutes or until breadsticks are golden.

Tied-Up in Knots

Italian Bread Knots: Substitute ¼ teaspoon dried Italian seasoning for cumin and chili powder. Sprinkle with 1 tablespoon grated Parmesan cheese. Proceed with recipe as directed.

Cajun Bread Knots: Substitute ½ teaspoon Cajun seasoning for cumin and chili powder. Add ¼ teaspoon dried thyme, if desired. Proceed with recipe as directed.

Whipped-Up
Sweet Inspirations

“Satisfy
your sweet tooth
with any of these
inspired desserts
that can be
whipped up in
a hurry!**”**

Black Bottom Banana Cream Pie

8 servings

prep: 12 minutes   chill: 2 hours

1   cup semisweet chocolate chips

1   (9") ready-made vanilla wafer pie
      crust
2   medium bananas, sliced

1   (3.4-ounce) package vanilla instant
      pudding mix
1   (3.4-ounce) package banana cream
      instant pudding mix
2½ cups milk
½   (8-ounce) container frozen whipped
      topping, thawed
2   (1.4-ounce) chocolate-covered
      toffee candy bars, coarsely
      chopped

1 Microwave chocolate chips in a small microwave-safe bowl at HIGH for 1½ minutes or until melted, stirring twice; set aside to cool slightly.

2 Spoon chocolate into pie crust. Arrange sliced bananas over melted chocolate.

3 Combine vanilla and banana cream pudding mixes in a medium bowl. Add milk, and whisk 2 minutes or until thickened. Pour over bananas; spread carefully with a spatula. Spread with whipped topping, and sprinkle with chopped candy bars. Cover and chill 2 hours.

"A layer of melted chocolate chips makes the black bottom of this creamy banana pie. And to make it even more tempting, we topped it with whipped topping and chopped candy bars. It's so-o-o satisfying!"

Mint Brownie Pie à la Mode

10 servings

prep: 8 minutes   cook: 28 minutes

½   cup sugar
¼   cup butter
1½ cups dark chocolate chips
2   large eggs, lightly beaten
⅔   cup self-rising flour
1   teaspoon vanilla extract
1   cup mint chocolate chips

Vanilla ice cream
Hot fudge sauce
Mint chocolate chips

1 Preheat the oven to 350°. Melt sugar and butter in a medium saucepan over medium heat. Remove from heat; stir in dark chocolate chips until melted. Add eggs and flour, stirring until just blended. Stir in vanilla and 1 cup mint chocolate chips. Pour into a greased 9" pie plate.

2 Bake at 350° for 28 minutes or until set. (Pie will not test done with a wooden toothpick.) Serve warm with vanilla ice cream and hot fudge sauce. Sprinkle with additional mint chocolate chips before serving.

"Mint, chocolate, and ice cream form an irresistible trio in this decadent dessert. I guarantee that it'll be a hands-down favorite with your gang!"

Orange Cream Pie

8 servings

prep: 15 minutes   freeze: 8 hours   cook: 7 minutes

4   cups (1 quart) ice cream, softened
1   (11-ounce) can mandarin orange
        segments, drained
1   (6-ounce) graham cracker crust
Orange Glaze (optional)
Garnish: orange rind curls

1 Beat softened ice cream and mandarin oranges at medium speed of an electric beater until blended. Spoon into pie crust. Cover and freeze 8 hours or until firm. If desired, serve with Orange Glaze, and garnish.

Orange Glaze

⅔   cup sugar
¼   cup water
3   tablespoons orange liqueur or
        3 tablespoons orange juice
2½   tablespoons light corn syrup
1   tablespoon grated orange rind

1 Bring all ingredients to a boil in a small saucepan, stirring constantly; boil 2 minutes. Cover glaze, and chill 1 hour. Yield: 1 cup.

TIME-SAVIN' TIP

Make this luscious pie the night before you plan to serve it. Then make and chill the glaze as you start dinner so it will be ready to serve with the pie after dinner.

Try this tip for super-neat servings: Run a knife under hot water for 1 minute before slicing the pie.

Tin Roof Pie

8 servings

prep: 14 minutes   freeze: 4 hours

2   cups coarsely crushed cornflakes
½   cup creamy peanut butter
½   cup light corn syrup

4   cups (1 quart) vanilla fudge swirl ice
      cream, softened
⅓   cup chocolate flavor syrup
½   cup chocolate-covered peanuts

1 Combine cornflakes, peanut butter, and corn syrup in a bowl. Press into a lightly greased 9" pie plate.

2 Spread softened ice cream evenly into crust. Drizzle with chocolate syrup; sprinkle with chocolate-covered peanuts. Cover and freeze at least 4 hours.

"This indulgent pie gets its name from the look of the swirled ice cream that's topped with chocolate syrup and chocolate-covered peanuts."

Caramel Apple Crisp

6 servings

prep: 15 minutes   cook: 22 minutes

3	(12-ounce) packages frozen apple chunks
3	tablespoons packed light brown sugar
1	teaspoon ground cinnamon
1	(13.4-ounce) can dulche de leche spread (see tip)
18	crunchy oatmeal cookies with raisins, crushed (about 2 cups crumbs)
2	tablespoons granulated sugar
¼	cup all-purpose flour
½	cup cold butter, cut into pieces

1 Preheat the oven to 375°. Microwave apples in a large microwave-safe bowl at HIGH for 11 minutes or until warm. Stir in brown sugar and cinnamon; spoon into a lightly greased shallow 2-quart baking dish. Spoon dulche de leche over apple mixture.

2 Combine cookie crumbs, granulated sugar, and flour in a medium bowl; cut in butter with a pastry blender until mixture resembles coarse crumbs. Sprinkle crumb mixture over apple mixture. Bake, uncovered, at 375° for 22 minutes.

Dulche de Leche

Dulche de Leche is Spanish for "sweet milk." It's sweetened condensed milk that's been caramelized to a thick and delicious spread. Look for it in the ethnic foods aisle or with other canned milks in the supermarket.

Apple Cheese Pizza

8 servings

prep: 13 minutes   cook: 15 minutes

2   tablespoons butter
3   large cooking apples, peeled, cored,
        and thinly sliced
¼   cup packed brown sugar
1   teaspoon ground cinnamon

1   (14-ounce) package prebaked Italian
        pizza bread shell
Nonstick butter-flavored cooking spray
1   cup (4 ounces) shredded sharp
        Cheddar cheese
½   cup chopped walnuts
Streusel

1 Preheat the oven to 450°. Melt butter in a large nonstick skillet over medium heat. Add apples; cook 6 minutes or until tender, stirring occasionally. Stir in brown sugar and cinnamon.

2 Meanwhile, place bread shell on a baking sheet; coat shell with cooking spray. Arrange apple mixture over shell. Sprinkle with cheese, walnuts, and Streusel.

3 Bake at 450° for 9 minutes. Serve immediately.

Streusel

⅔   cup all-purpose flour
⅓   cup sugar
½   teaspoon ground cinnamon
⅓   cup cold butter, cut into pieces

1 Combine first 3 ingredients in a large bowl; cut butter into flour mixture with a pastry blender until crumbly. Yield: 1½ cups.

A is for Apple

Apples are available year-round but are at their peak September through November. They come in red, yellow, or green and vary in taste from tart to sweet. The most common apples to use for cooking are Braeburn, Granny Smith, McIntosh, Rome Beauty, and York.

Rustic Apple-Cranberry Tart

8 servings

prep: 15 minutes   cook: 30 minutes

2   (12-ounce) packages frozen
           escalloped apples

½   cup sweetened dried cranberries
6   tablespoons brandy (see tip)
2   tablespoons water
¼   cup packed light brown sugar
⅓   cup plus 3 tablespoons all-purpose
           flour, divided

⅓   cup packed light brown sugar
¼   cup cold butter
⅓   cup chopped walnuts

1   (15-ounce) package refrigerated pie
           crusts

Simple Substitutions
To make this tart kid-
friendly, just substitute 6
tablespoons apple juice
concentrate for the brandy.

1 Preheat the oven to 400°. Thaw apples in microwave at MEDIUM (50% power) 6 to 7 minutes.

2 Microwave cranberries, brandy, and 2 tablespoons water in a large microwave-safe glass bowl at HIGH 2½ minutes; stir in apples. Add ¼ cup brown sugar and 3 tablespoons flour, stirring to blend. Set aside.

3 Combine remaining ⅓ cup flour and the ⅓ cup brown sugar in a bowl; cut in butter with a pastry blender until crumbly. Stir in walnuts.

4 Unfold pie crusts; stack on a lightly floured surface. Roll into a 15" circle. Place on a lightly greased baking sheet. Spoon apple mixture in center of pastry, leaving a 3" border. Sprinkle with walnut mixture. Lift pastry edges, and pull over apple mixture, leaving a 9" circle of fruit showing in center. Press folds gently to secure.

5 Bake at 400° on lower oven rack for 30 minutes.

Chocolate-Banana Cream Tarts

4 servings

prep: 5 minutes

1   medium banana, thinly sliced
4   mini graham cracker pie crusts
2   (3.5-ounce) chocolate pudding cups
1   (1.4-ounce) chocolate-covered
     toffee candy bar, crushed

1 Arrange banana slices evenly in pie crusts. Spoon pudding over bananas. Sprinkle evenly with crushed candy.

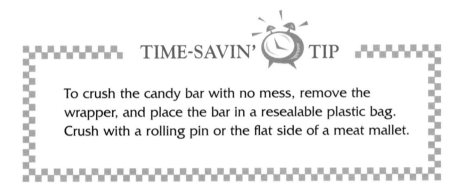

TIME-SAVIN' TIP

To crush the candy bar with no mess, remove the wrapper, and place the bar in a resealable plastic bag. Crush with a rolling pin or the flat side of a meat mallet.

Chocolate Cookie Pudding

6 to 8 servings

prep: 10 minutes   chill: 5 minutes

1   (5.9-ounce) package chocolate
      instant pudding mix
2   cups milk

1   (3-ounce) package cream cheese,
      softened
1   (8-ounce) container frozen whipped
      topping, thawed

16   double-stuffed cream-filled
      chocolate sandwich cookies,
      crushed
¾   cup chopped pecans, toasted

1 Whisk together pudding mix and milk for 2 minutes. Cover and chill 5 minutes.

2 Meanwhile, stir together cream cheese and whipped topping.

3 Place 1 cup crushed cookies in an 8-cup bowl. Spread half the cream cheese mixture on top; sprinkle with half the toasted pecans. Spread all the pudding over top; spread remaining cream cheese mixture over pudding. Sprinkle with remaining cookies and pecans. Cover and chill until ready to serve.

Scrumptious Substitutions

Mocha Cookie Pudding: Crush 16 coffee-flavored cream-filled chocolate sandwich cookies. Stir 2 tablespoons strong coffee into cream cheese mixture. Omit pecans. Proceed with recipe as directed.

Chocolate-Peanut Butter Cookie Pudding: Crush 16 peanut butter cream-filled chocolate sandwich cookies. Substitute ¼ cup peanut butter for cream cheese and 1 cup chopped dry-roasted peanuts for pecans. Proceed with recipe as directed.

Peach Trifle

8 to 10 servings

prep: 15 minutes   chill: 1 hour

1   (9") round angel food cake
⅓   cup orange juice

2   cups milk
1   (3.4-ounce) package vanilla instant
      pudding mix
1   (12-ounce) container frozen
      whipped topping, thawed

6   fresh ripe peaches, peeled and
      coarsely chopped

1 Cut cake horizontally into 3 layers. Brush orange juice over cake layers. Cut into 1" cubes.

2 Combine milk and pudding mix in a medium bowl. Beat 30 seconds with a wire whisk. Let stand 2 minutes or until thickened. Fold in 2 cups whipped topping.

3 Layer half each of cake cubes, peaches, and pudding mixture in a 3-quart trifle dish or glass bowl. Repeat layers. Top with remaining whipped topping. Cover and chill 1 hour.

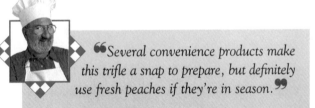

❝Several convenience products make this trifle a snap to prepare, but definitely use fresh peaches if they're in season.**❞**

Maple-Walnut Pears

4 servings

prep: 10 minutes   cook: 12 minutes

1   tablespoon butter
1½   teaspoons vegetable oil
4   firm pears, peeled, cored, and
            cut in half lengthwise (see tip)

3   tablespoons maple syrup
2   tablespoons brown sugar
1   tablespoon finely chopped walnuts

Vanilla ice cream

1 Melt butter in a large nonstick skillet over low heat; add oil. Increase heat to medium-high. Place pear halves, cut sides down, in pan. Cook 3 minutes or until golden.

2 Reduce heat to medium; add maple syrup and brown sugar. Cook 6 minutes or until pears are tender. Remove from heat; stir in nuts.

3 To serve, place 2 pear halves on each of 4 dessert plates; drizzle each evenly with remaining syrup mixture in pan. Top each with ice cream. Serve dessert immediately.

Pear Prep
Bosc or red Bartlett pears are recommended for this recipe because their sturdier shape holds up well when cooked. To prevent discoloration, peel and cut pears just before cooking.

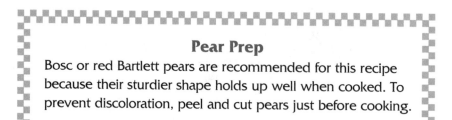

California-Style Peach Melbas

4 servings

prep: 10 minutes

1	(10-ounce) package frozen strawberries in light syrup, thawed
1½	tablespoons red currant jelly
1⅓	cups vanilla frozen yogurt
2	large ripe peaches, peeled and sliced (see tip)
1	cup fresh raspberries
½	cup frozen whipped topping, thawed

1 Place strawberries with syrup in a blender; process 20 seconds.

2 Place jelly in a custard cup; microwave at HIGH 25 seconds. Stir into strawberry purée.

3 Spoon ⅓ cup frozen yogurt into each of 4 serving dishes. Drizzle each serving with 5 tablespoons strawberry mixture, and top evenly with peaches and raspberries. Dollop each serving with 2 tablespoons whipped topping. Serve immediately.

TIME-SAVIN' TIP

To speed up preparation, use 1½ cups frozen peaches, thawed, instead of 2 fresh peaches.

Cookies 'n' Cream Parfaits

4 servings

prep: 7 minutes

¼ cup chocolate flavor syrup
1 tablespoon coffee liqueur (optional)

1 cup chocolate or vanilla ice cream
4 cream-filled chocolate sandwich
    cookies, crumbled
1 cup coffee ice cream

1 Combine chocolate syrup and, if desired, liqueur in a small bowl, stirring well with a whisk.

2 Place ¼ cup ice cream into each of 4 glasses. Drizzle with 1½ teaspoons chocolate syrup mixture and about 2 tablespoons crumbled cookies. Spoon ¼ cup coffee ice cream over crumbs in each glass, and top with remaining syrup mixture and cookies.

"If you don't want to use the liqueur, just leave it out. You'll still get that rich chocolate-coffee flavor from the syrup and coffee ice cream."

Chocolate-Mint Sundaes

4 servings

prep: 5 minutes

12   (0.25-ounce) chocolate-covered peppermint patties

2   tablespoons milk

Vanilla ice cream

1 Place peppermint patties and milk in a small microwave-safe glass bowl. Cover; microwave at HIGH 1 minute or until patties melt, stirring every 15 seconds. Serve over ice cream.

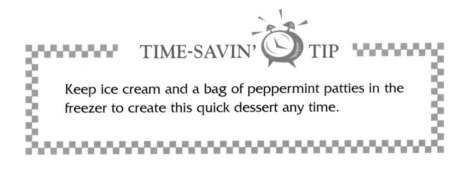

TIME-SAVIN' TIP

Keep ice cream and a bag of peppermint patties in the freezer to create this quick dessert any time.

Elegant Cookie-Cream Torte

10 to 12 servings

prep: 14 minute   freeze: 4 hours

2   (3-ounce) packages ladyfingers, split

1   (1.75-quart) container cookies and
       cream ice cream, slightly softened
¾   cup hot fudge sauce
1½   cups coarsely crumbled cream-filled
       chocolate sandwich cookies (about
       15 cookies), divided
½   (8-ounce) container frozen whipped
       topping, thawed

1 Stand ladyfingers, cut sides in, around
edge of a 9" springform pan; line bottom of pan with remaining ladyfingers.

2 Spoon ice cream into lined pan, and
spread evenly. Drizzle fudge sauce
over ice cream, and sprinkle with 1 cup
crumbled cookies. Spread whipped topping over cookies, and sprinkle with
remaining ½ cup crumbled cookies.
Cover and freeze at least 4 hours.

*"Impress the gang with this elegant torte for dessert.
They'll think you worked all morning when all you
did was assemble some very tasty convenience products.
Shhh . . . they never have to know!"*

Peanut Butter and Ice Cream Sandwich Dessert

8 to 10 servings

prep: 15 minutes   freeze: 4 hours

1   (16-ounce) can chocolate flavor
        syrup
1   cup chunky peanut butter

19   chocolate ice cream sandwiches
1   (12-ounce) container frozen
        whipped topping, thawed and
        divided
6   (1.5-ounce) packages peanut butter
        cup candies, chopped and divided

1 Combine chocolate syrup and peanut butter in a medium microwave-safe bowl. Microwave at HIGH 1½ minutes or until melted, stirring after 45 seconds; cool.

2 Layer 9½ ice cream sandwiches in a 9" x 13" pan. Spread with half the whipped topping; drizzle with half the chocolate syrup mixture. Swirl together with a knife; sprinkle with half the chopped candies. Repeat layers, ending with remaining chopped candies. Cover and freeze 4 hours.

"Wanna know a secret? Ice cream sandwiches make up the chocolaty cake layer of this devilishly good—and easy—dessert."

Candy Bar Pizza

10 to 12 servings

prep: 10 minutes   cook: 18 minutes

1   (18-ounce) package refrigerated
     sliceable chocolate chip cookie
     dough

2   cups frozen whipped topping,
     thawed
2   (2.7-ounce) chocolate-coated
     caramel-peanut nougat bars,
     coarsely chopped
2   (1.4-ounce) chocolate-covered
     toffee candy bars, coarsely
     chopped
2   (2.1-ounce) chocolate-covered
     crispy peanut-buttery candy bars,
     coarsely chopped
¼   cup caramel topping

1 Preheat the oven to 375°. Press cookie dough onto a greased 12" pizza pan. Bake at 375° for 15 to 18 minutes. Cool completely.

2 Spread whipped topping evenly over cookie dough. Sprinkle chopped candies over whipped topping. Drizzle lightly with caramel topping. Refrigerate pizza until ready to serve. Cut into wedges to serve.

❝This dessert pizza is studded with chopped candy bars and drizzled with buttery caramel—making it the ultimate treat for a children's party!❞

Banana Crêpes with Chocolate-Hazelnut Sauce

3 servings

prep: 8 minutes   cook: 7 minutes

½   cup hazelnut chocolate spread
¼   cup evaporated milk
1   teaspoon vanilla extract

¼   cup butter
¼   cup packed light brown sugar
4   large firm bananas, sliced

6   ready-made crêpes (see tip)
Powdered sugar

1 Combine chocolate spread and milk in a small saucepan over medium heat; stir until smooth. Stir in vanilla; keep warm.

2 Meanwhile, melt butter and brown sugar in a large nonstick skillet over medium-high heat. Add bananas; cook 2 minutes or until softened.

3 Spoon bananas evenly down center of crêpes. Fold sides over, and place seam side down on serving plates. Spoon sauce over crêpes; sprinkle with powdered sugar. Serve immediately.

TIME-SAVIN' TIP

Look for prepackaged crêpes near the fruit in the produce section of larger supermarkets.

Peanut Butter and Chocolate Cheese Ball

(pictured on facing page)

1 (4") cheese ball

prep: 9 minutes   cook: 2 minutes   chill: 2 hours

1   (8-ounce) package cream cheese,
    softened
¼   cup butter, softened
¼   cup creamy peanut butter

¾   cup powdered sugar
2   tablespoons light brown sugar
3   tablespoons unsweetened cocoa
½   cup chocolate and peanut butter
    chips
1   tablespoon chocolate liqueur
    (optional)

⅔   cup finely chopped pecans, toasted
Graham crackers

1 Beat cream cheese, butter, and peanut butter at medium speed of an electric beater until creamy.

2 Stir in sugars, cocoa, chips, and if desired, liqueur. Cover and chill 2 hours or until firm.

3 Shape chilled mixture into a ball, and roll in toasted pecans. Serve with graham crackers.

❝Who says a cheese ball has to be savory? Jazz up things at your next party with this sweet version. It's great served with graham crackers or apple and pear slices.❞

Triple Chocolate Mocha
Cookies and Brickle 'n'
Chip Cookies,
pages 185 and 188

Dark Chocolate-Mint Brownies,
page 199

Caramel Apple Cupcakes

(pictured on facing page)

2 dozen

prep: 15 minutes   cook: 20 minutes

1   (18.25-ounce) package spice cake
       mix
1   cup chopped Granny Smith apple
       (about 1 large)

35   caramels
¼   cup evaporated milk

½   cup chopped peanuts
24   wooden craft sticks

1 Preheat the oven to 350°. Prepare cake mix according to package directions; stir in apple.

2 Spoon batter into paper-lined muffin pans, filling two-thirds full. Bake at 350° for 20 minutes or until a wooden toothpick inserted in center comes out clean; remove to a wire rack to cool.

3 Meanwhile, combine caramels and milk in a medium saucepan over low heat; stir 4 minutes or until smooth.

4 Spread caramel mixture over cupcakes; immediately sprinkle with peanuts, pressing in slightly. Insert a wooden stick into center of each cupcake. Store covered in an airtight container.

"These cupcakes will be a hit at your next bake sale! Wrap them in cellophane to carry out the caramel apple theme."

Blueberries 'n' Cream Cake

12 to 15 servings

prep: 8 minutes   chill: 2 hours

8   vanilla cream-filled snack cakes

1   (8-ounce) package cream cheese,
        softened
2   cups sifted powdered sugar
2   (8-ounce) containers frozen
        whipped topping, thawed
1   (21-ounce) can blueberry pie filling

1 Slice cakes in half lengthwise; place in a single layer in a 9" x 13" baking dish.

2 Beat cream cheese and sugar at medium speed of an electric beater until smooth, about 1 minute. Fold in 1 container of whipped topping; spread mixture over cakes. Spoon pie filling over cream cheese mixture. Spread with remaining container of whipped topping. Cover and chill at least 2 hours before serving.

Cherries 'n' Cream Cake
Substitute cherry pie filling for blueberry for a different flavored dessert. And a sprinkling of chopped nuts on top gives this version a nice rich crunch.

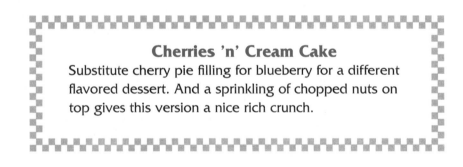

Carrot-Raisin Snack Cake

12 to 15 servings

prep: 15 minutes   cook: 30 minutes

1½ cups packed light brown sugar
½ cup butter, softened
2 large eggs
1 teaspoon vanilla extract

1½ cups all-purpose flour
½ teaspoon baking soda
½ teaspoon salt
½ cup chopped raisins
1½ cups finely grated carrots
½ cup pecans or walnuts, finely
      chopped

1 Preheat the oven to 350°. Beat brown sugar and butter at medium speed of an electric beater until creamy; add eggs and vanilla, beating well.

2 Stir in flour, baking soda, and salt just until moistened; stir in raisins and carrots. Spread mixture into a lightly greased 9" x 13" pan. Sprinkle with pecans.

3 Bake at 350° for 30 minutes or until a wooden toothpick inserted in center comes out clean. Cool on a wire rack, and cut into squares.

TIME-SAVIN' TIP

This is a great dessert to keep on hand by making and freezing it for later use. Simply line the bottom of the pan with parchment paper and lightly dust with flour; then proceed as directed in the recipe. After cake has baked, cool for 10 minutes, and then remove from the pan—the cake should slide out easily. Once completely cooled, wrap cake in plastic wrap, and then wrap again in heavy-duty aluminum foil. Cake can be frozen up to 3 months.

Fluffy Cream Cheese Fruit Dip

3 cups

prep: 10 minutes

1   (8-ounce) package cream cheese,
    softened
2   cups powdered sugar
2   teaspoons vanilla extract
½   cup whipping cream, whipped

1 Beat cream cheese, powdered sugar, and vanilla at medium speed of an electric beater until fluffy. Fold in whipped cream; serve with fresh strawberries.

Citrusy Dips

Citrus-Cream Cheese Dip: Add 1 tablespoon grated lime, lemon, or orange rind to cream cheese mixture. Proceed with recipe as directed.

Smooth Orange-Cream Cheese Dip: Add ¼ cup orange liqueur to cream cheese mixture. Proceed with recipe as directed.

Orange Marmalade-Cream Cheese Dip: Add ½ cup orange marmalade to cream cheese mixture. Proceed with recipe as directed.

Pineapple and Banana-Rum Salsa

2½ cups

prep: 10 minutes   cook: 3 minutes

2   medium-sized firm bananas, peeled
        and halved lengthwise
2   (8-ounce) cans pineapple chunks in
        juice, drained
3   tablespoons light brown sugar

1   tablespoon butter, softened
1   teaspoon ground cinnamon
2   tablespoons dark rum or
        ½ teaspoon rum extract
1   teaspoon vanilla extract
Vanilla ice cream

1 Preheat the broiler. Place banana halves and pineapple chunks on a lightly greased baking sheet; sprinkle with brown sugar.

2 Broil 5½" from heat 3 minutes or until sugar is bubbly. Let cool slightly.

3 Coarsely chop bananas. Combine bananas, pineapple, butter, cinnamon, rum, and vanilla in a large bowl; gently toss to combine. Serve warm over ice cream.

Salsa Servings

Try this fruity salsa over your next batch of homemade waffles for a fresh alternative to syrup. It's also a tasty topping for pound cake or angel food cake.

Mocha Fudge Sauce

1¾ cups

prep: 7 minutes

2   cups semisweet chocolate chips
1   tablespoon butter

½   cup whipping cream
¼   cup strong brewed coffee

1 Place chocolate chips and butter in a heavy saucepan. Cook over low heat until chocolate and butter melt, stirring often.

2 Gradually add whipping cream, whisking constantly. Cook, stirring constantly, 2 to 3 minutes or until smooth. Remove from heat; stir in coffee. Serve warm over ice cream.

"In the time it takes to open a jar of commercial fudge sauce and heat it up, you can make our homemade version. With its hint of mocha flavor, this velvety sauce is a winner over your favorite ice cream. What are you waiting for?"

Fast-Bakin' Confections

"Indulge the gang—and yourself— with a batch of these delectable cookies and candies. They bake up fast and disappear just as quickly!**"**

Chocolate-Cherry Cookies

about 2½ dozen

prep: 12 minutes   cook: 14 minutes per batch

1   (18.25-ounce) package devil's food
         cake mix
¼   cup water
1   large egg, lightly beaten
¼   cup butter, melted

1   (5-ounce) package dried cherries,
         chopped
2   cups white chocolate chips
⅔   cup chopped pistachios

1 Preheat the oven to 350°. Beat first 4 ingredients at medium speed of an electric beater until smooth.

2 Fold in cherries, white chocolate chips, and pistachios.

3 Drop by heaping teaspoonfuls 2" apart onto lightly greased baking sheets. Bake at 350° for 14 minutes or until set. Remove to wire racks to cool.

Winning Pair

Chocolate and cherries are as natural together as champagne and caviar or peanut butter and jelly. Try these and see—or taste—for yourself!

Triple Chocolate Mocha Cookies

(pictured on page 174)

about 3 dozen

prep: 13 minutes   cook: 11 minutes per batch

1   (18.25-ounce) package devil's food
     cake mix
¼   cup strong brewed coffee
1   tablespoon coffee liqueur (optional)
¼   cup butter, melted
1   large egg, lightly beaten

½   cup chocolate chunks
½   cup milk chocolate chips
½   cup white chocolate chips

1 Preheat the oven to 350°. Beat first 5 ingredients at medium speed of an electric beater 2 minutes, stopping to scrape down sides.

2 Fold in chocolate chunks, milk chocolate and white chocolate chips.

3 Drop dough by heaping teaspoonfuls 2" apart onto lightly greased baking sheets. Bake at 350° for 11 minutes or until set. Remove to wire racks to cool.

"These cookies with 4 hits of chocolate score big! A hint of coffee and coffee liqueur add even more great flavor."

Chewy Fudge Cookies

about 2 dozen

prep: 15 minutes   cook: 10 minutes per batch

2   cups semisweet chocolate chips,
        divided
2   (1-ounce) unsweetened chocolate
        squares, chopped
2   tablespoons butter

2   large eggs, lightly beaten
⅔   cup sugar
¼   cup self-rising flour
1   teaspoon vanilla extract
1   cup chopped pecans, toasted

1 Preheat the oven to 350°. Combine 1 cup chocolate chips, the unsweetened chocolate, and butter in a medium saucepan over low heat, stirring until melted. Remove from heat.

2 Stir in eggs, sugar, flour, and vanilla with a wooden spoon until combined. Stir in remaining 1 cup chocolate chips and the pecans. Drop by heaping teaspoonfuls 2" apart onto lightly greased baking sheets.

3 Bake at 350° for 10 minutes or until edges are done. Remove from pans; cool completely on wire racks.

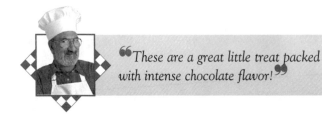

"These are a great little treat packed with intense chocolate flavor!"

Crispy Praline Cookies

about 2 dozen

prep: 10 minutes   cook: 15 minutes per batch

1   cup all-purpose flour
1   cup packed dark brown sugar
1   large egg
1   cup chopped pecans
½   cup butter, softened
1   teaspoon vanilla extract

1 Preheat the oven to 350°. Stir together all ingredients in a large bowl, blending well. Drop dough by tablespoonfuls 2" apart onto ungreased baking sheets.

2 Bake at 350° for 13 to 15 minutes. Cool on baking sheets 1 minute; remove cookies to wire racks to cool completely.

TIME-SAVIN' TIP

Let the butter sit at room temperature for several hours, or soften it in the microwave at HIGH for 10 to 20 seconds (do not melt).

Brickle 'n' Chip Cookies

(pictured on page 174)

about 3 dozen

prep: 13 minutes   cook: 9 minutes per batch

1   (14-ounce) can sweetened
        condensed milk
½   cup chunky peanut butter
2   cups biscuit baking mix
1   teaspoon vanilla extract
1   cup semisweet chocolate chips
½   cup almond toffee bits

½   cup sugar

1 Preheat the oven to 375°. Combine condensed milk and peanut butter in a large bowl. Beat at medium speed of an electric beater until creamy. Add biscuit baking mix and vanilla, beating just until blended. Stir in chocolate chips and toffee bits.

2 Shape dough into 1" balls; roll in sugar. Place 1" apart on lightly greased baking sheets.

3 Bake at 375° for 8 to 9 minutes or until lightly browned on bottoms. Remove to wire racks to cool.

"You'll go nuts for these cookies. They're quick to make and, of course, delicious to eat—my kind of recipe!"

Lemon Crisps

about 4 dozen

prep: 12 minutes   cook: 9 minutes per batch

1   (18.25-ounce) package lemon cake
        mix with pudding
1   cup crisp rice cereal
½   cup butter, melted
1   large egg

1 Preheat the oven to 350°. Combine all ingredients, stirring mixture well.

2 Shape dough into 1" balls; place about 2" apart on ungreased baking sheets.

3 Bake at 350° for 9 minutes or until edges are golden. Cool on baking sheets 1 minute; transfer to wire racks to cool completely.

"Four ingredients are all it takes to whip up these crispy cookies! And thanks to the lemon cake mix, we have a nice lemony flavor without squeezing fresh lemons."

Easy Orange Cookies

about 4 dozen

prep: 5 minutes   cook: 10 minutes per batch

1   (18.25 ounce) package orange cake
    mix
2   cups frozen whipped topping,
    thawed
1   large egg, lightly beaten
⅓   cup finely chopped macadamia nuts
Powdered sugar

1 Preheat the oven to 350°. Combine first 4 ingredients in a large bowl, stirring well. Shape dough into balls, using 1 teaspoon dough for each; roll in powdered sugar. Place 2" apart on greased baking sheets.

2 Bake at 350° for 10 minutes or until edges are golden. Cool 1 minute on baking sheets; remove to wire racks to cool completely.

TIME-SAVIN' TIP

These simple-to-make cookies start with a cake mix and end with 4 dozen melt-in-your-mouth delights.

Peanut Butter-Kiss Cookies

about 3 dozen

prep: 10 minutes   cook: 11 minutes per batch

1   (14-ounce) can sweetened
        condensed milk
¾   cup peanut butter
2   cups biscuit baking mix
1   teaspoon vanilla extract

¼   cup sugar

1   (13-ounce) package milk chocolate
        kisses, unwrapped

1 Preheat the oven to 350°. Beat condensed milk and peanut butter at medium speed of an electric beater until creamy. Add biscuit baking mix and vanilla, beating at low speed just until blended.

2 Shape dough into 1" balls; roll in sugar. Place 2" apart on lightly greased baking sheets.

3 Bake at 350° for 11 minutes. Remove from oven, and immediately place a chocolate kiss in center of each cookie. Remove cookies to wire racks to cool.

These chocolate-kissed cookies sure catch your attention. They're love at first bite!

Almond Spice Bars

about 2½ dozen

prep: 5 minutes   cook: 25 minutes

1   (18.25-ounce) package spice cake
      mix
2   tablespoons sugar
2   large eggs
½   cup butter, melted
1¼ cups water
½   cup chopped slivered almonds,
      toasted

Orange Glaze

1 Preheat the oven to 375°. Combine first 5 ingredients in a large bowl. Beat at medium speed of an electric beater until blended. Stir in almonds. Pour into a greased 10" x 15" rimmed baking sheet.

2 Bake at 375° for 20 to 25 minutes or until a wooden toothpick inserted in center comes out clean. Cool slightly. Drizzle with Orange Glaze. Cut into bars.

Orange Glaze
1½ cups sifted powdered sugar
3   tablespoons orange juice

1 Combine sugar and orange juice, stirring until smooth. Yield: ½ cup.

TIME-SAVIN' TIP

This cakelike bar cookie recipe starts with a convenient cake mix and ends with an easy 2-ingredient glaze. You can substitute carrot cake mix for the spice cake mix if you prefer.

Raspberry Bars

about 32 bars

prep: 8 minutes   cook: 26 minutes

1   (18.25-ounce) package yellow
        cake mix
2½   cups quick-cooking oats, uncooked
¾   cup butter, melted
1   (12-ounce) jar raspberry preserves

1 Preheat the oven to 375°. Combine cake mix and oats. Stir in butter until mixture is crumbly. Press about 3 cups mixture into a greased 9" x 13" pan. Spread preserves over crumb mixture. Sprinkle with remaining crumb mixture. Pat gently to level topping.

2 Bake at 375° for 24 to 26 minutes or until golden. Cool completely in pan on a wire rack. Cut into bars.

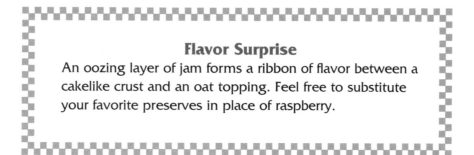

Flavor Surprise
An oozing layer of jam forms a ribbon of flavor between a cakelike crust and an oat topping. Feel free to substitute your favorite preserves in place of raspberry.

Chocolate-Peanut Bars

about 4 dozen

prep: 10 minutes   cook: 3 minutes   chill: 1 hour

1   cup butter, softened
1   cup chunky peanut butter
1   (16-ounce) package powdered
        sugar
1½ cups vanilla wafers, crushed
        (about 45 cookies)

2   cups semisweet chocolate chips
½   cup whipping cream

1 Beat butter and peanut butter at medium speed of an electric beater until blended. Add powdered sugar and vanilla wafer crumbs; beat until blended. Press mixture into a lightly greased 9" x 13" pan lined with wax paper.

2 Stir together chocolate chips and whipping cream in a medium saucepan over low heat until melted and smooth. Spread over peanut butter mixture. Cover and chill 1 hour or until firm.

3 Remove from refrigerator, and let stand at room temperature 10 minutes or until slightly softened. Cut into bars.

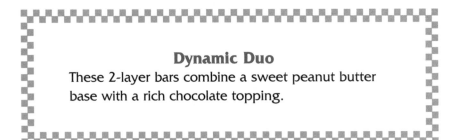

Dynamic Duo
These 2-layer bars combine a sweet peanut butter base with a rich chocolate topping.

Coconut-Pecan Bars

about 2 dozen

prep: 10 minutes   cook: 25 minutes

1   (18-ounce) package refrigerated
      sliceable sugar cookie dough

1   (14-ounce) can sweetened
      condensed milk
2   cups semisweet chocolate chips
1⅓ cups flaked coconut
1   cup chopped pecans

1 Preheat the oven to 350°. Press cookie dough in a lightly greased 10" x 15" rimmed baking sheet.

2 Pour condensed milk over dough; spread evenly. Sprinkle with chocolate chips, coconut, and pecans; press down slightly. Bake at 350° for 25 minutes or until golden. Cool completely on a wire rack. Cut into bars.

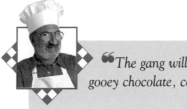

"The gang will love this—a sugar cookie crust heaped with gooey chocolate, coconut, and pecans!"

Strawberry Cheesecake Bars

about 2 dozen

prep: 10 minutes   cook: 30 minutes

1   (18.25-ounce) package strawberry
      cake mix
½   cup butter, melted
1   large egg, lightly beaten

1   (8-ounce) package cream cheese,
      softened
1   (16-ounce) package powdered
      sugar
2   large eggs, lightly beaten
1   teaspoon vanilla extract

1 Preheat the oven to 375°. Combine cake mix and butter in a large bowl. Add 1 egg; stir well. Press into a lightly greased 9" x 13" pan.

2 Beat cream cheese, powdered sugar, and 2 eggs at medium speed of an electric beater until creamy; stir in vanilla. Pour cream cheese mixture over crust.

3 Bake at 375° for 30 minutes or until just set; cool completely on a wire rack. Cut into bars.

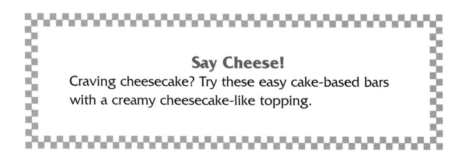

Say Cheese!
Craving cheesecake? Try these easy cake-based bars with a creamy cheesecake-like topping.

Tortoni Squares

about 9 servings

prep: 15 minutes   freeze: 8 hours

⅓ cup chopped toasted almonds
3 tablespoons butter, melted
1⅓ cups finely crushed vanilla wafers
1 teaspoon almond extract

½ gallon vanilla ice cream, softened
1 (12-ounce) jar apricot preserves

1 Combine almonds, butter, vanilla wafer crumbs, and almond extract; press ⅓ mixture into a buttered 5" x 9" loaf pan.

2 Spread half the ice cream over crumb layer. Repeat layers once, and top with preserves. Press remaining crumb mixture on top. Cover and freeze 8 hours or up to 1 month. Let stand 10 minutes before cutting into squares and serving.

TIME-SAVIN' TIP

Make this dessert up to a month ahead, freeze it, and relax! Your special dessert's done—what could be simpler?

Drop Brownies

about 4 dozen

prep: 15 minutes   cook: 7 minutes per batch

2   cups semisweet chocolate chips
1   (14-ounce) can sweetened
         condensed milk
½   cup butter
1   cup all-purpose flour

1 Preheat the oven to 350°. Combine first 3 ingredients in a medium saucepan; cook over low heat, stirring constantly, until melted. Stir in flour.

2 Drop dough by rounded teaspoonfuls 2" apart onto ungreased baking sheets. Bake at 350° for 7 minutes. (Cookies will be soft; do not overbake.) Cool on baking sheets 2 minutes; remove to wire racks to cool completely.

"Chocolate chips, butter, flour, and sweetened condensed milk are all you need to prepare these drop-dead delicious, chewy fudge brownie-like cookies."

Dark Chocolate-Mint Brownies

(pictured on cover and page 175)

about 2 dozen

prep: 10 minutes   cook: 29 minutes

1   (21-ounce) package chewy fudge
      brownie mix
3   cups special dark chocolate chips,
      divided

1½ cups powdered sugar
½   cup sour cream
1   teaspoon vanilla extract
1   (4.67-ounce) package chocolate
      mints, chopped

1 Preheat the oven to 350°. Prepare brownie mix according to package directions; stir in 2 cups dark chocolate chips. Pour brownie mixture into a lightly greased 9" x 13" pan. Bake at 350° for 29 minutes or just until brownies pull away from sides of pan; cool completely.

2 Meanwhile, melt remaining 1 cup dark chocolate chips in a medium-size microwave-safe bowl in microwave at HIGH for 1½ minutes or until melted, stirring after 45 seconds.

3 Add powdered sugar, sour cream, and vanilla to chocolate; beat at medium speed of an electric beater until smooth. Spread over brownies; sprinkle evenly with chopped mints. Cut into squares.

TIME-SAVIN' TIP

Use the bag chocolate mints that are already chopped. You'll find them in the baking section of your grocery store.

Peanut Butter Brownies

about 2 dozen

prep: 15 minutes   cook: 28 minutes

1   (21-ounce) package chewy fudge
     brownie mix
½   cup coarsely chopped dry-roasted
     peanuts
2   cups semisweet chocolate chips

¼   cup butter, softened
2   tablespoons creamy peanut butter
2   cups sifted powdered sugar
2   tablespoons milk
1   teaspoon vanilla extract

1 Preheat the oven to 350°. Prepare brownies according to package directions, stirring in peanuts and chocolate chips. Spread brownie mixture into a lightly greased 9" x 13" pan. Bake at 350° for 28 minutes or until brownies pull away from sides of pan; cool completely on a wire rack.

2 Meanwhile, beat butter and peanut butter at medium speed of an electric beater until creamy. Add powdered sugar, milk, and vanilla; beat until smooth. Spread frosting over cooled brownies. Cut into squares.

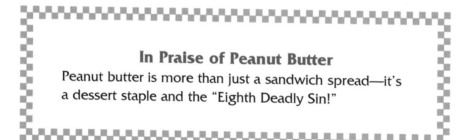

In Praise of Peanut Butter
Peanut butter is more than just a sandwich spread—it's a dessert staple and the "Eighth Deadly Sin!"

Chocolate-Peanut Clusters

about 2½ dozen

prep: 10 minutes   cook: 10 minutes   chill: 10 minutes

1   cup butterscotch chips
1   cup semisweet chocolate chips
2   tablespoons creamy peanut butter
2   cups salted Spanish peanuts

1 Place first 3 ingredients in a heavy saucepan. Cook over low heat, stirring constantly, until smooth. Remove from heat; stir in peanuts.

2 Drop by rounded teaspoonfuls onto a baking sheet lined with wax paper. Chill 10 minutes before serving. Store in refrigerator.

TIME-SAVIN' TIP

Lining baking sheets with wax paper makes cleanup a snap, and that means more time to enjoy goodies like these nutty treats!

Chocolate Chip-Cream Cheese Cups

about 2 dozen

prep: 14 minutes   cook: 13 minutes

1   (18-ounce) package refrigerated
     sliceable chocolate chip cookie
     dough

1   (8-ounce) package cream cheese,
     softened
3   tablespoons sugar
1   teaspoon vanilla extract
½   teaspoon lemon juice
Chocolate candy sprinkles (optional)

1 Preheat the oven to 350°. Shape dough into 1" balls. Press into miniature (1¾") muffin pans.

2 Bake at 350° for 13 minutes. Immediately make indentations in center of each by lightly pressing with the handle of a wooden spoon. Cool in pans 5 minutes; remove to wire racks to cool completely.

3 Meanwhile, beat cream cheese and sugar at medium speed of an electric beater until smooth. Stir in vanilla and lemon juice. Spoon evenly into cookie cups; sprinkle with chocolate candy sprinkles, if desired. Keep refrigerated until ready to serve.

TIME-SAVIN' TIP

Forget making pastry—use handy refrigerated cookie dough to line muffin cups for these bite-sized treats.

Mocha-Pecan Fudge

about 2 pounds

prep: 8 minutes   chill: 2 hours

1 tablespoon instant coffee granules
2 teaspoons hot water

2 cups semisweet chocolate chips
1 (14-ounce) can sweetened
    condensed milk
1 teaspoon vanilla extract
1 cup chopped pecans, toasted

1 Line a 9" square pan with aluminum foil; lightly coat with nonstick cooking spray.

2 Combine coffee and water until coffee is dissolved; set aside.

3 Combine chocolate chips and condensed milk in a medium saucepan over low heat, stirring until smooth. Stir in coffee, vanilla, and pecans. Spread mixture evenly into prepared pan. Cover and chill at least 2 hours. Cut into bars.

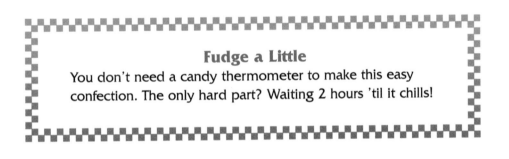

Fudge a Little
You don't need a candy thermometer to make this easy confection. The only hard part? Waiting 2 hours 'til it chills!

METRIC EQUIVALENTS

The recipes that appear in this cookbook use the standard United States method for measuring liquid and dry or solid ingredients (teaspoons, tablespoons, and cups). The information in the following charts is provided to help cooks outside the U.S. successfully use these recipes. All equivalents are approximate.

EQUIVALENTS FOR DIFFERENT TYPES OF INGREDIENTS

A standard cup measure of a dry or solid ingredient will vary in weight depending on the type of ingredient. A standard cup of liquid is the same volume for any type of liquid. Use the following chart when converting standard cup measures to grams (weight) or milliliters (volume).

Standard Cup	Fine Powder	Grain	Granular	Liquid Solids	Liquid
	(ex. flour)	(ex. rice)	(ex. sugar)	(ex. butter)	(ex. milk)
1	140 g	150 g	190 g	200 g	240 ml
¾	105 g	113 g	143 g	150 g	180 ml
⅔	93 g	100 g	125 g	133 g	160 ml
½	70 g	75 g	95 g	100 g	120 ml
⅓	47 g	50 g	63 g	67 g	80 ml
¼	35 g	38 g	48 g	50 g	60 ml
⅛	18 g	19 g	24 g	25 g	30 ml

DRY INGREDIENTS BY WEIGHT

(To convert ounces to grams, multiply the number of ounces by 30.)

1 oz	=	¹⁄₁₆ lb	=	30 g
4 oz	=	¼ lb	=	120 g
8 oz	=	½ lb	=	240 g
12 oz	=	¾ lb	=	360 g
16 oz	=	1 lb	=	480 g

LENGTH

(To convert inches to centimeters, multiply the number of inches by 2.5.)

1 in					=	2.5 cm		
6 in	=	½ ft			=	15 cm		
12 in	=	1 ft			=	30 cm		
36 in	=	3 ft	=	1 yd	=	90 cm		
40 in					=	100 cm	=	1 meter

LIQUID INGREDIENTS BY VOLUME

¼ tsp					=	1 ml		
½ tsp					=	2 ml		
1 tsp					=	5 ml		
3 tsp	=	1 tbls			=	½ fl oz	=	15 ml
		2 tbls	=	⅛ cup	=	1 fl oz	=	30 ml
		4 tbls	=	¼ cup	=	2 fl oz	=	60 ml
		5⅓ tbls	=	⅓ cup	=	3 fl oz	=	80 ml
		8 tbls	=	½ cup	=	4 fl oz	=	120 ml
		10⅔ tbls	=	⅔ cup	=	5 fl oz	=	160 ml
		12 tbls	=	¾ cup	=	6 fl oz	=	180 ml
		16 tbls	=	1 cup	=	8 fl oz	=	240 ml
		1 pt	=	2 cups	=	16 fl oz	=	480 ml
		1 qt	=	4 cups	=	32 fl oz	=	960 ml
					33 fl oz	=	1000 ml	= 1 liter

COOKING/OVEN TEMPERATURES

	Fahrenheit	Celsius	Gas Mark
Freeze Water	32° F	0° C	
Room Temperature	68° F	20° C	
Boil Water	212° F	100° C	
Bake	325° F	160° C	3
	350° F	180° C	4
	375° F	190° C	5
	400° F	200° C	6
	425° F	220° C	7
	450° F	230° C	8
Broil			Grill

Index

FAVORITE RECIPES

Jot down the family's and your favorite recipes here for handy-dandy, fast reference.
And don't forget to include the dishes that drew oohs and aahs when you had the gang over.

Recipe	Source/Page	Remarks